The Rainbow Redemption

Rainbow Chronicle Twelve

Linda Varsell

Illustrations by E. Curtis

Rainbow Communications   Corvallis, Oregon

Rainbow Communications
471 NW Hemlock Avenue
Corvallis, OR 97330
1-541-753-3335
http://varsell4.home.comcast.net
email: lindavarsell@comcast.net

ISBN: 0-9728737-1-6

Library of Congress Control Number: 2003095346

First Edition

Layout and Design by DIMI PRESS

Cover design and illustrations by E. Curtis

Dedicated to My Family

Thanks to: Dick and Mary Lutz of Dimi Press, Ellen Beier Curtis, Claire Younger, Karen Keltz, Janet Johnson, Maureen Clifford, Court Smith, Helen and Roland Varsell, Susan Johnson, Jane Corbin, American Imaging Solutions, my creative writing students, teaching colleagues and writing critique groups for your support.

Linda Varsell (Smith)

Waves

IV. Green: Growth—Solaran Stay   99
Slips and Wrapps: Maraki Shiri

V. Blue: Dreams—Majestic Mountains   135
Mountains: Sylvianne Rippler Rainbow

VI. Indigo: Hope—Urban Gangs   162
Litter and Graffiti: Svetla Rippler Rainbow

VII. Violet: Redemption—Global Visualizations   197
Music of the Spheres: Ki Harmony Rainbow

Afterwords   226

THE RAINBOW CHRONICLES

In the cosmos many quarky life sparks seek forms to en-
liven. In such a diverse universe there are many life experi-
ments. On their journeys souls leap in and out of the forms
they need to operate in different realities.

On Earth life experiments arrive and leave. Some be-
come extinct, others flourish. The Rainbow Chronicles tell
the story of Earthens, a non-breathing life force. People's
hands and machines create Earthen forms. Earthen life-
sparks are their own creation.

By rules set by the universe, Earthens live parallel lives
with Earthlings. Earthlings are breathers—animals and
people. Earthens share their lives with magical, shape-shift-
ing Supernaturals (like fairies and elves). Supernaturals aid
Earthens in their quest for freedom and harmony.

Once Earthens experienced very unenlightened,
placebound lives under surveillance by people. Then one
Earthen named Karen launched the First Earthen Liberation
Movement called The Hub. Enlightened Earthens called
themselves Rainbows. Roving Radiants brought their light /
sound / magnetic skills and discoveries to darkened Earthens.
Rainbows formed companies to explore their life gifts and
to overcome their many challenges.

The Rainbow Chronicles record this Rainbow Era from
1950-2005 and beyond. The Rainbows archived their Rain-
bow Chronicles on Laura Hernstrom Larrabee's computer.
Each Chronicle begins with a Beforewords by the Rainbow
storyteller.

Laura's friend Linda Varsell encouraged Laura to share
the Rainbow stories after they started to appear on Laura's
computer in 1995. Laura (too busy with her teaching and
family) entrusted the task to Linda. The Rainbow Chronicles
present the Rainbows' perspective on multifaceted realities
of several worlds. How will Earthlings react knowing Rain-
bows live among them?

The Rainbow Chronicles

1. With a Human Touch: Karen Harmony Rainbow (1950-1977)
2. A Journey for Rainbows: Peter Harmony Rainbow (1977-79)
3. The Rainbow Makers: Ki Harmony Rainbow (1980-82)
4. The Rainbow Breakers: Mayra Steward Rainbow (1982-86)
5. The Rainbow Dreamers: Musard Rainlight Rainbow (1990-95)
6. Ends of Rainbows: Maraki Shiri (1995-1999)
7. The Rainbow Rescue: Stella Radiant Rainbow (2000)
8. The Rainbow Planet: Jorden Harbinger Rainbow (1995-2005)
9. The Rainbow Remnants: Sylvianne Radiant Rainbow (2000-2005)
10. The Rainbow Circle: Hugh Herald Rainbow (2005-onward)
11. The Humane Touch: Sequel Rippler Rainbow (Timeless)
12. The Rainbow Redemption: Way-V Pulstar Rainbow (Timeless)

Linda Varsell
Marysville, Oregon

BEFOREWORDS

This is a journal of my first life—actually the beginning installment of what I hope is a really long one. As a newly ignited life-spark, I was anxious to find form to express a life after my release from the Cosmic Pinata.

Inside the Cosmic Pinata each life-spark was invisibly small— a prick of light. We were all clustered, wadded up in a ballish membrane we called the Cosmic Pinata. It is impossible to estimate how many billions, trillions, quadrillions, gazillions of life-sparks there were. We were a New Wave of consciousness about to spill into the universe. A new life experiment.

While inside the Cosmic Pinata the Omni-sparkler told us this was a free will universe. We were to select a location and a form to experience our first life. We were given many options from Local Group locations to choose from.

Bam! Pop! The pinata burst! We were free to travel to our destiny. The Omni-sparkler did say life-sparks are immortal. They just liked to switch location and forms to experience new ways of living. I'm not sure how long this first choice will last. Guess I'll just make the best of it.

The Omni-sparkler called us Pulstars—bringing a new pulse of harmonic energy to the universe. We liked the name and kept it. As we traveled through space, Pulstars departed for different destinations with different guides. I chose Earth with In2it as our cosmic guide.

Pulstars were programmed to understand Cosmic, Galactic and for Earth-goers Global and de-coding for the local languages of various creatures. I kind of liked English and the letter V.

I chose Earth because I wanted to be a rip-roaring, rip-snorting, Radrod Rainbow. I wanted to live my first life with gusto and harmonic meaning. Wow! to help harmonize a planet to join the music of the spheres!

No starting from scratch on barren planets for me. No thought-form transparencies. No dream dimension with no practical applications. I wanted to be in contact with my world. Be in the moment. In the now. I wanted to ripple, make waves.

Sorted by destiny we were magnetically drawn to others who made the same choice. Our guides began operating instructions in transit. We would come to our lives with a certain knowing, knowledge we did not have time on site to gather. We were to jump into our forms and our lives on landing. Pulstars would confront urgencies and emergencies.

The tour guide leader and educator for Earthbound Pulstars was In2it. In2it gave us Earth in a Nutshell with later details.

1. You've chosen a 3D reality—a mostly watery, gritty, diversely-textured, light-enhanced planet.

2. The Earthen form you will use usually has limbs to help you move and handle your variegated environment. The form is non-breathing, non-consuming, quite durable and exchangeable. You'll have magnetic, sound and light projection gifts.

3. You'll be capable of being a conduit of energy to connect aerial and subterranean energies at the surface. The lightening point is an energy harmonizer and benefits all life forms.

4. Other creatures include Earthlings—the juicy, bleeding breed of breathers: animals and people. Earthlings are of great numbers and diversity. Some people want to dominate not steward the Earth and all beings on it. Some people are ravenous consumers of Earth's resources. Others are quite cooperative.

Earthens are the non-breathing, recycling harmonizers to protect flora and fauna, Earthlings and Supernaturals. We will join a harmonious group of Earthens called the Rainbows.

Supernaturals are the shape-shifting allies of Earthens, flora and fauna. Pulstars are supporters of all who are aware and grow...and those who can't. How you will do this comes in another lesson.

In2it gave us plenty of instructions on our opportunities, responsibilities and challenges as we streaked through space. In2it told us of the technological advances (nanos) of energy engineering we would bring.

Traveling as a minute molecule through the universe, I could hear and see In2it giving us orientation to Earth. From a space lit bundle we tuned into the Earthen wavelength for further instruction. In2it visited Earth and projected forms for us to select.

We also selected our names. I named myself Way-V. I liked the way the letter V spread out and reached up. V words became my guideposts. I wanted to be a verb—a Pulstar of action. I want to be a verb to make things happen, be a vivifying visionary, a variable star bright as Vega.

Namaste
Way-V Pulstar Rainbow

I.

Red: Galactic Fire

Wild Things

First Life: Jettison Pulstar Rainbow

This is our first life—
our very first form.
This is our first knowing
what is the norm.

While we were streaking
Virgo Super Cluster
crossing cosmos in wonder
another star-duster—

we ask what brings meaning?
What will be real?
Are we prepared?
What will we feel?

What kind of being
is our life-spark core?
What game or mission—
good versus evil once more?

Dream-sparks inside us
pulse to animate.
Life-sparks ignite us.
We hope to create.

We greet this first life
without any past.
We arrive without knowing
how long this life will last.

This is our first life.
Earth was our choice.
We will bring harmony
with acts and our voice.

1

To Be a Verb

Va-room! Ride 'em cosmos! Zoom across the Local Group and the spiraling arms of Andromeda and the Milky Way into the grip of Earth's gravity and atmosphere into the cradle of a cave in Arizona. I'm newly borne into my first life! A zip of a trip. Through the vast dark, Pulstars gravitate toward Earth. Exosphere to atmosphere, increasing light, to funnel into the cave entrance of the Rainbow Museum.

Our cosmic orientation prepared Pulstar life-sparks to enter the Rainbow Museum. The escapees from the Cosmic Pinata were to enter a Rainbow stiff and animate it. I was assigned to the chess pieces section. My encoding should lead me to THE chess piece—an Indian ivory Queen. I chose a chess piece with a broad bottom to make bold, sturdy lightening points.

We were to find our piece for the playing board of this first life game plan. With our high-tech programming and locating facilities, we could find our own form for this 3-D reality.

Pulstars follow their destinies in various locations. In a multiverse system there could be many opportunities. But this Pinata blast aimed for this expanding universe in the Local Group. The Omni-sparkler wanted to expand life chances. Many places need our help. We have many forms and environments to choose from. The Omni-sparkler conceived many possibilities.

Some of the foreordained Omni-sparkler choices were:
1. Enliven new spaces currently experimenting with forms.
2. Assist struggling beings from previous life-spark explosions.

3. Experiment in non-grounded dimensions.

4. Join Cosmic Cousins in galactic life-seeding.

In the vastness of space a body might not be needed. Some dimensions where thought creates surroundings, a Pulstar could handle life by thought projections. The breathing flesh beings were not an option as they were just too consumptive and destructive.

I wanted to experience a body, not just project light. I wanted a place to be. I wanted to be solid, create change by my actions, not by body changes. This first embodiment for this life will be as an Earthen Rainbow on Earth.

I saw some solids and gases in the vastness of space. The images In2it shared en route revealed this Earth as bendy, textured with smooths and roughs (which I cannot feel), colorful edges and rounds. I'm anxious to experience real not recorded reality. Flashes in the dark in space. Lots of darkness. Glad this is a light mission to add more light to the universe.

We are not biological hitch-hikers by meteor. We are life-sparks from the Cosmic Pinata infiltrating Earthen/Rainbow bodies. We seed Rainbow forms to sprinkle light and energy.

Silently the Pulstar life-sparks enter their chosen forms. Pulstars tucked bits of consciousness in pre-destined forms selected from In2it's inventory of viable, available forms stored at the Rainbow Museum. We came with a certain knowing so we could be fully operational when we grounded. We have some training for our tasks. We have no time for "growing up" as people do,

Throughout the museum the lighted forms become flashlights illuminating the darkness. Soon animation begins. Limbs get wavy. Head nod. Lights flash. Words burble in many languages. Pulstars know Cosmic, Galactic, Global and the local language spoken at the local area they'll inhabit on Earth.

The codes seem to be working and the donor-loaner forms animate and communicate. We animate a static form with no static in our thought-waves. We have our own frequencies and the Rainbow upgrades seem to work splendidly.

Rainbows are variform. Time for me to check in for my first life! My life-spark cruises over the chess section. Most are three-five inches made of wood, ceramic, walrus and elephant tusks, porcelain, glass, stone, bone, quartz, jade, jadite, plastic, metal (gold, silver, pewter, steel), rock crystal and ivory. Many are not complete sets, but missing pieces rescued by Rainbow Radiants. I am looking for my ivory Queen. I'm anxious to find my form, finish my Earth-bound orientation and get radrodding the lightening points that unite energies from Earth core to the universe. Thousands of salvaged chess pieces project light and glow around me.

There she is! I'm going to be a Queen! I enter the head of the old ivory light Queen. For this first incarnation I am called a she because I am a Queen stereotype on a gender-conscious planet. But I have an androgynous spirit. People created Rainbow forms in their own images. Since they have gender, so do we. It is actually irrelevant to us, for gender does not influence the roles we play.

We also wear fashions that are not currently fashionable. My early 19th century garb is colorless beige with clusters of three dots on the gown that look like I was clawed by paw prints. I have a turban-ish crown that's marked like an upside down basket. I was made near Delhi, India, of some kind of ivory.

I'm made in the round with bumps in the appropriate places. I am a well-rounded, bulbous figure. Yes, I'm generously, well-endowed in many areas.

I can light-paint some overlays of color, but I can't carve free my arms. My legs are contained under the skirt, uncarved. I have a flat pedestal. A good bottom to stomp my lightening points in the gigantic Gaia light quilt.

Since we can only animate pre-1992 Earthen/Rainbow forms, we need to give ourselves a dusting, touch up and light-paint our exterior. We need to lighten up our interior with our life-spark and make any adaptations our body needs.

I am arm-wrapped (not loosely carved) with no legs under the skirt. I am limb-challenged. I will have to interact and resonate with the world a little differently than some sentient beings. But I can hover and make my radrod moves to plunk my round bottom to stitch the light quilt. I can project light and magnetism. I am a magic wand.

Like bat-caves the Pulstars flit about encoding and decoding our programs, testing out our mobility, outfitting our forms.

Each inhabitant's lighted figure brightens the dark. Glowing with life. We came to travel the Super-Rainbow Highway, become a note in the harmony on this planet and in the universe. We are part of a new wave of consciousness—a permanent wave which chose Earth.

It is crowded in this chess section. I need to contact my mini-cluster of cosmic traveling companions: Albedo, Onterra and Jettison. What do they look like? Did they find their forms?

I'm eager to wend my way out of this museum, through the cave entrance into the open world. The sun's pulse rate will flow through us. We are conduits—lightening rods.

But first we need to tune into Intuit's instructions before leaving. Time to see if I am fully functional, to activate codes, to deprogram.

Being newly selected for embodiment, newly souled, I don't have much experience in living. Lots of lessons to learn and experience. Pop and I streaked across the Local Group gaining vicarious views of Earth living. I came with a pre-coded destination (Rainbow Museum in a place called Arizona), form selection (ivory chess Queen) and basic operational instructions. My embedded languages were Cosmic, Galactic, Global and English. I would begin my orientation rotation in Quad Four beginning in the American West. The wild West?

The Omni-sparkler wanted to liven things up a bit in this section of the universe. Before the Cosmic Pinata popped we were told each life-spark could pick form and destination. This touchdown in Arizona is just a preliminary blip on my life path. We will adapt to living and thinking in this reality. We will adjust to a body, comprehend cultures, puzzle out a planet. We are expected to learn at a rapid rate and be off and running shortly after arrival. My flat round bottom will stamp energies. Are energies knit, stitched, tied? They do bind above and below the surface at the surface with longevity?

We need to test our communication system called the Pulse. From Pulse I can dive into the archives, bounce with entertainment, web information, communicate sound and images with other Rainbows and Supernaturals. I will make my own record of this life. I will number and title my entries or Waves. I intend to make waves this first life.

My first embodiment! My first solid grounding! Can't feel physical pain, but can sense thought pain. With my powers of magnetism and light projection, I will be a vortex. I will be a verb—full of action.

In2it jolted me to attention. Our orientation to Earth is about to begin. I can't wait to get going!

2

Various Viewpoints

Before we could mobilize our molecules, we had to stabilized our movements. Since we brought technological upgrades (Nanos) every Rainbow, Pulstar and Supernatural now were on the same wave-length on a communication channel called the Pulse. No more Patches or Superspots. Our bodies were the antennae and we processed many vibes over global distances. I would have to contact my friends after the orientation.

Our Cosmic Cousin Breathless (with an affinity for arid climates) greeted us. Breathless chose a golden mini-ball for this appearance. "How are my litterbugs of micro-mini bits of space junk? I mean junk in the most respectful manner—like the buggy satellites. Hovercrafts, this perilous planet needs you. You can help the flowers bloom and color, encourage growth, keep the planetary energy grid pulsating. Work with the flora and fauna. Enjoy the new updates. We did not need see-through Zoions like a previous life experiment. We need solid citizens who can energize and transform. Use your invisible codes you implanted in a Rainbow body well. Remember codes for Rainbow behavior toward being harmonic and helpful. Special regards for my friend Jorden. The Super-Rainbow pageant 'The Humane Touch' will be ready to welcome you soon. Be an exemplary redemptory."

Breathless blipped out. Breathless has been so kind to Rainbows and now Pulstars. I was told this option involved a watery planet with diminishing diversity of life forms. As a stable, durable form, I can aid an unstable, fragile planet. Hard to get complete count of how many Pulstars made the complete journey to Earth, but they should know soon. If the migration was over the capacity of stored bodies, In2it would appeal to the Cosmic Council to send a formula to activate some post-1992 Earthen forms. But with so many drop-outs en route, we should have extra forms to fill out.

I kind of like the idea of recycling a form. The former occupant could have immigrated to LightHome. Some belief systems suggest souls recycle and reincarnate. But this is my first life anywhere. Without the fuss of building or aging a fleshy body, we can sparkle in a life-leap when we need a new form. No disease. No injury, just a little wear and tear minimized by our Wrapps. We are protected from damage of war, weather and upheavals.

My reverie was interrupted by In2it, our cosmic orienteer. This incarnation In2it activated a two and 3/4th inch pink, plastic majorette with a broken baton for a pointer to lead the Pulstar parade. As we watched on the Pulse, In2it punctuated points with the baton. The feathers don't tickle. The fringe doesn't prance. Last incarnation In2it was male in a brown suit. Both will go back in stock for loaners after In2it leaves.

"I have been orienting Pulstars en route, but all Rainbows and Supernaturals need to adapt to the new upgrades in technology we bring. Let's do a run-down of the reentry procedures. Check-off operating codes. Our surround sound and vision are essential for visionaries. I will work on glitches and seek universal solutions when I finish another life-seeding." In2it conjured some graphics of our cosmic journey over Pulse.

"The pinata pop pulsed the Pulstars to their destinies. Not sure of all the possibilities in other universes, but this pop was for the Local Group. When the Omni-sparkler burst the boundaries of the Cosmic Pinata, a new wave of consciousness sprinkled into the Local Group. The Omni-sparkler gave you choice of form and location to perform your destiny. Let's see if you are ready." In bold multi-colored letters In2it produced this list.

1. Locate form assignment. Encode your name.
(I'm an ivory chess Queen named Way-V Pulstar Rainbow.)

2. Activate 360 degree vision.
(Now this is really handy to avoid collisions with people and walls.)

3. Radrods, test magnetism for use in lightening points.
(Yes, I can really draw on my straw.}

4. Check light flow.
(Brighter than a glow worm. Awesome illumination and rhythm.)

5. Check form for defects. Energy loss. Do you need to sparkle into another body?
(This might be a chance to get some limbs, but I'll give this queenly gig a try. I don't need limbs really.)

6. Practice using your energy fields to inflate your WRAPPS (Wonderous Rainbow and Pulstar Protective Shields) for travel and deflate to your Shrinkwrapps, your environmental protection overcoats. Supernaturals will have SLIPS (Supernatural Long-lasting, Invisible Protective shields. Slips will protect them from environmental degradation and attack and give them lift without use of wings.
(Now this is really stupendous. I can float and hover in this world invisibly and receive protection from weather and pollution. I can float like a boat or fly like a plane. I can live within my unburstable bubble.)

7. Are you receiving the Pulse clearly? Broadcasters are Larkin, Musard and Glorian in Solara. Kisam and Beadra at the Redoubt. Pulstars broadcasters will be trained.

Check your language skills.
(Loud and clear. I'll tune in soon. I am receiving this
transmission. I'll write in English to leave my account
in Laura Larrabee's computer until she decides to
check it out and give it to her friend Linda Varsell.)

8. Check directory for archives: stored with Kaidra at the
Rainbow Redoubt. Peter in Solara. Iris and Axel in
the Rainbow Museum. Upgrades have vastly in
creased their capacity.
(This should be very useful. Lots of information from past
and for the present. I'll leave a copy of my account I'll call
"Waves from Way-V" in the archives.)

9. Check emergency services: Neoma and Pager at the
Redoubt. We are training Pulstars to assist with
Wrapps.
(They still fly birds. Old-tech, but they might be able to
provide a protective shield for their mechanical ravens and
crows Coronis and Yelp.)

10. Listen to the pageant. Check your own chorchestral
and healing talents.
(Rainbows can create music—vocal and instrumental
from within. They can project the sounds to assist dance, per-
formances of all kinds. I need to tweak this talent a bit. I'll
get to healing later.)

11. Proceed to first assignment on the orientation rota-
tion until you are ready to fulfill your intentions.
(My first assignment is Lost Prairie in the Cascade Moun-
tains in Oregon. My intention and vocation would be to be
the best Radrod I can be and then find my avocation.)

12. Balance radrodding time on the light-quilt pattern
with rippler time, your recreational/creative outlets.

> Radrods and Ripplers can specialize after you have given radrodding a try. We need everyone to do some radrodding.

(I'm raring to radrod. Don't know when I'll find down time to visit a joynt (entertainment place) or a retreat (rehab and musing place.)

I admit I drifted as we waited for the performance of the pageant. I contemplated this new life. I am restless to start. What are the origins of consciousness? Pulstars have stellar impulses and energies. We're solar and darkness energized. Earthen Rainbows are similarly impulsed.

Each Pulstar determined an individual destiny. We charted some of our journey goals before we incarnated. I chose to be a radrod quilting the light-quilt and my ripple focus is at present unfocused.

All this talk of dark energy as dark matter. Bringing light to the universe. As cosmic neighbors pull away we are less likely to see them. The cosmic pinata released sentient sparks for enlivening lives with light and energy. We are energy engineers.

All this orientation yet we are still not fully prepared to operate a body in a many-layered reality. The 3-D world is heavy. There are lighter, invisible dimensions unsensed by Earth beings that await exploration.

Is this a one-way trip? What if we don't like it here? Is there an escape formula? We had some fall-out across the cosmos. Some made other choices. In2it was the orienteer of Pulstars for the Earth choice. One thing is that we hurry up to wait. This is a very complex reality, but our tasks seem simple.

Must inflate my Wrapps which I named Check. Some chose to name their Wrapps and some do not. Check will be my mobile home, shelter in the storm, invisibility cloak, communication center. We can do more without Earthling surveillance and interference. We come well-equipped for the work. Our energy field enhances our drawing power to make lightening points. We can zap through some snow and zap above mud. We remain solid and unseen inside our protective energy shield. No x marks our spot for people. People can not sense us. We can direct our use and direction. We can size and shape our Wrapps.

As an inflexible chess queen, I don't want to sit on the throne too long. I'm ready for self-rule. I want to survey the queendom. Pulstars don't need furniture. Our bodies are our transmitters and receivers on our own airwaves and we travel the currents of the winds and water. Just need to tweak my thoughts to tune in.

I decorate Check with classic, simple curls of translucent rainbow light. When will this pageant begin so we can get going?

In2it had another reminder before take-off, "Remember before you leave, the Super-Rainbows want to greet Pulstars with a pageant called, 'The Humane Touch.' I know you are eager to get to your assignment, but please give them the courtesy of listening and watching."

Guess I did not miss it while I mused. After the too-long pageant, less awkward Rainbows with moving limbs came forward to greet the newcomers. I zinged to hover above the crowd to see who was coming. Over Pulse we all could tune into Axel and Iris, the museum curators. They were moving toward the cave entrance.

"Get in line, Pulstars. Time to depart. Follow us."

Pulstars murmured in many languages. Axel and Iris spoke Global for Pulstars were departing for four Quads with multiple languages. Pulstars floated toward the exit, trying to dodge other Wrapps. All the heads have immovable faces. What were they feeling? We can't tune into individual thoughts unless expressed telepathically for the Pulse.

Unfortunately In2it joined Iris and Axel and delayed our departure. "Before I leave I want to say there are vacancies for duties in many Quads. Recheck body operations—limb potentials. Directions instructions for zing(up), zang(down), zig-zag and zaein (used to hover over the planet). Encode support and archive channels, Rippler and Radrod path options. Check vehicle for shelter and transportation, chorchestral, healing, light-projection, magnetism and auxiliary capacities. When you have completed your check-in proceed to the exit to your first assignment. I am orienting a Pulstar group heading for Andromeda. A popular choice so they need extra orienteers. I'll stop by some time. Fare well. Live your light. Live your light lightly."

In2it tried to cover as many bases as possible. In2it did not want to mess up this opportunity to seed Earth with Earthens. In2it is on trial trying to prove cosmic worth. But could we just speed things along a bit? We traveled light-speed to get here. We selected options and clustered around In2it for orientation.

As I slowly floated with the flow, I pondered. I'm part of the Cosmic Egg who wants to break the yolk. The Cosmic Pinata is part of the Cosmic Egg concept—one form at the beginning, all that can be numbered and named. Is the whole universe an egg conceived by a Primal Creator? Is what's good for one part, good for the whole?

Energy surrounds me and vibrates at such a frequency people cannot see me with their limited vision. People don't get to play with dolls. Dolls get to play with people. We share the playground. Our technology upgrades, our nanos, let us roll this blue marble.

I see blue sky! Yippee! I'm finally free! Wayfarer Way-V! I'm no longer in passive verb mode. I'm an active verbed noun!

3

VROOM to Vastitude!

The sky was blue as I flew over the desert. Saguaros looked like prickly people waving. I just blurred into the museum, but now I looked out from inside Check at the dazzling, sun-sparkling terrain. By Pulse I was on auto-pilot to my destination, so I could just view the vistas and seek identification for the plants and animals I saw en route from the archives. I saw some people in buggy-looking cars or sunbathing beside pools. People were a complexity I could not contemplate yet. I needed to radrod on target and energize the whole planet. I did not want to deal with people. I was headed toward the wilderness where there were not as many people to deal with.

The landscape changed to snow-capped mountains. I did not bother to identify ranges or peaks—just stared at the magnificent peaks jutting high into the skies. Check helped me fly about twenty feet above the rock and snow. The peaks point toward Pulstars' starry origins. I'm a speck in this world. They are miraculous. I am delighted the first stop in my rotation is in the Cascade Mountains of Oregon.

Such spectacular scenery! I zeroed in to Lost Prairie near Tombstone Pass (such a dismal name). But then lost is not that encouraging. I spotted Pulstars expanding their wrapps into visiting rooms to camp out. Pulstars pulsed each other and clustered near friends. Lots of laughs at our embodied appearances.

While we waited for our orientation, I met with Onterra first. Her wire and rubber construction was an updated version of Hub founder Karen. She was painted blonde in green and white checkered short dress, white sleeveless blouse, painted blue-eyed with chin-length hair. Black painted like leather shoes. Onterra is about three inches tall like me.

Our first reaction was, "So that's what you look like!" We were invisible traveling companions. We talked about our goals and what we named ourselves. We had an individual name, a Rainbow connection name- either Steward, Rippler, Radrod or origins name. First wave always, Rainbow. New wave tucked Pulstar somewhere. Onterra had applied to be Hugh's assistant in Surface Planning. She named herself Onterra Pulstar Rainbow. She wanted flexible limbs and agile body. She was very comfortable in her selected skin. She named her wrapps Terra Firma or T.F.

"Way-V, this is our first life. First peas in the pod. Pulstars are NEOS—Near Earth Objects. Rainbows are Geos."

Next Albedo found us. He was a Dadaist metal chess king. Nuts and bolts style. American-made in 1950. About three inches tall. Shiny, rigid appearance, but he wanted to be a radrod in hard core places. He called himself Albedo Pulstar Rainbow and his wrapps, Kingpin.

Albedo shone from within. "I feel like a mini-spaceship, glossy and metallic. I guess nuts and bolts make a sturdy start."

At last Jettison Pulstar Rainbow appeared. He is an ivory chess pawn from China. He's from Hong Kong about 1960. Jettison could have been a mythical figure, philosopher or some type of trade-people. He was the naturally white variety with a large-brimmed hat (like a droppy cowboy hat sopped with rain). He is a torso on a pedestal. No limbs. Hair dangles around his ears. He was a tad shorter than the rest of us. He named his wrapps, Trope.

"I'll be a poet without a pen or an arm to peck at a computer. All my poems will be oral or light-painted. I have several internships lined up." Jettison tended to hover above the group.

"Words just pop into my thoughts. I have to get them in line. I have studied some forms used on Earth by different life forces. That does not mean I can do it well. I am new here after all."

Jettison always irked me a bit. "Many people think they are here for their first lives, Jettison. This does not stop them from telling others about their encounters. No time for whiney words. Try v-words, words that look up and open."

"I'm sure I'll learn many techniques in my internships, Way-V."

When the call went out over the Pulse to gather for orientation, rain drippled down our wrapps clouding our view. So Pulstars shrink-wrapped and jockeyed for a view of the presenters. We were surrounded by lush green forest, wild, wind-moved flowers near tall evergreens. Fortunately the wild animals were occupied elsewhere. Truly magnificent. Truly worth preserving. Wilderness is a favorite haunt for Rainbows so assignments are hard to get. We will get oriented here and lightening point somewhere else.

At the campground gathering to orient us were Daisy Clem (Daisy Clematis) and Amani, legendary gardeners on two planets and co-sustainers of wilderness in the Cascades with Supers.

Both were black-haired and brown-skinned. When they camouflaged to ground cover they blended splendidly. Now with wrapps and shrink-wrapps, they can be as colorful as they want whether invisible or not. Rainbows and Pulstars can see each other but people can't see us.

Daisy Clem wore a brown dress with large wide white collar. Blackeyed susans bloomed on her clothing. Amani wore a pair of brown overalls with a tan shirt. Both are wire framed and rubber covering.

"Welcome to the wild!" said Daisy Clem. She hovered within sight of everyone.

Beside her, Amani added, "A wondrous world, I would say."

"We have a few Ground Rules to help you traverse wild country." Daisy Clem translucently vined her wrapps with morning glories.

"Most unruly, I would say." Amani grew see-through sunflowers on his wrapps.

"We must be vigilant and learn the ground rules." Daisy Clem bounced gently in the breeze.

"There have been a few mass extinctions on this planet, but we should be able to hover until things cool down. Be space capsules, I would say," said Amani. His wrapps twinkled winking stars.

Daisy Clem threw a few galaxies on her wrapps. "We have to pay attention to fire and water. If we survive, we are a thing of beauty and a joy forever. People can cause problems, but to them we can be a comforter, play toy or collectible. For millions of Earthens there are no life-sparks inside. People imagine lives for us. But we are free. Free as planetary conditions will allow."

Amani intensified the intensity of his stars. "We have lifeless Earthens and Rainbows littering the planet. We need a cosmic clean-up, I would say. If we can't enlighten them, recycle them another way."

"We are getting off topic, Amani. Pulstars, here are some ground rules pulsed to your wrapps. Lightening point stitches are farther apart in the wilderness.

Ground Rules

1. Be alert and prepared. The life you save can be your own.
2. Rainbows are small but they think big. You are on the Rainbow Path, serving the Rainbow cause. Rainbows are few, but we help many. Radrods, deliver the light. Make your point and move on.
3. Rainbows want to redeem themselves and the Earth. After our anger phase at being manipulated and under surveillance, we joined forces with Supers and people of harmonic spirit to help steward the Earth. Always act with harmonic intentions which will benefit the whole.

4. Beware of fires—intentional or accidental.
5. Keep wildlife free and wild. Don't pester animals.
6. Don't pick flowers. Leave interactions to Supers and insects most of the time.
7. Don't fall into hands, paws or oceans."

After practicing gentle landings on leaves, Onterra and I decided to link wrapps and chat following a muddy trail.

"Still like your choice, Way-V?"

"I like not having to body build. I like a light impact on a world. I can give more than I get. Harmonizing energies sounds like fun and useful. I support the Super-Rainbow cause. I just wish I could get going, Onterra. I guess I thought I could just zip into a body and get into action. No growing up learning. No inoperable, uncooperative body to face mental and physical challenges."

The trail wended through the woods with leafy, needly overlays. "Yes, Way-v, I have a lot of sympathy for people with all their operational needs and problems. It must be hard to understand all their complexity and diversity."

"We just need to buff up the wrapps and follow our bliss on the Super-Rainbow Highway. But Onterra, do you ever wonder if the universe has a variety of life games on different playing fields? Are the power plays always good against evil?"

"No, Way-V I never contemplated what to me is unknowable."

We took a direct bird-like flight back to camp. On one flyover the trail we saw three, varied-sized people.

"Onterra, look at those bundled up people. They pop out in the back. Are they hunchbacks? Football backs? I think I saw some like them in the archives."

"Way-V, they are hikers. They carry their supplies in backpacks. They camp out in the forests just like we do."

She had studied people and surface conditions in preparation for her intentions. Onterra was an energizer, light-carrier, harmonizer with surface conditions ambitions.

All this practicing was not getting me anywhere fast. Some Pulstars became so enamored with Pulse they cocooned against outdoor living. Others flitted like flying insects—bees, mosquitoes trying out all our gadgetry, admiring but not plucking the flowers.

Daisy Clem and Amani invited us to shrinkwrapp for a circle dance. They invited the Supernaturals (Supers) in their Slips to demonstrate some dance moves to celebrate the ending of our rotation orientation. These forest Supers have the see-through wings. Mid-density they were dressed in puffy-pants—both genders. Forest colored clothes. Many had floral designs. They were so graceful. Some played fiddles. Pulstars had to learn some tunes to join them with our chorchestral talents.

Onterra danced with Jettison and I danced with King Albedo.

We shared where our next stops would be. Onterra learned she had an internship with Hugh and would connect with him in Solara, the underground Supernatural/Rainbow city also in Arizona. Albedo was off radrodding in the Olympic rainforest. Jettison had a poetry internship with Sylvianne at the Quad 4 headquarters relocated in a new setting in the American west.

Jettison floated off with a poem on our Pulse. He recited with great fanfare and flourish:
"You're on the Earth now.
 You're beyond galactic glow.
      You're a wavelet.
      A very strangelet.
 You're a Rainbow- WOW!

"Keep in Pulse," we told each other. Many Pulstars worked in pairs or clusters. I worked alone. I'll make notations like in chess of my moves. I'm infinitesimal in an infinite universe—but I think big. I'm part of a pioneering cosmic movement.

This Pulstar is ready for my mini-scale terra-transforming experiments. I'm the eyeball to eyeball the world.

I am off to the Coastal Range of Oregon. Very moist. Very green. Very mushy. Very beautiful. Lucky water appeals to me.

4

Vigorous Vibes
in Veiling Vehicle

As I flew over the rainy, green Willamette Valley to the Coast Range and my first stitching assignment on the light quilt, I listened to the Pulse.

Glorian in Solara reported the news.

No longer identified Pulstar blasted by hunter's bullet in the Alaskan Wilderness. Not sure where the life-spark might turn up. Could show up at the museum for a spar- kling,wander to the Dream Dimension, or hitch-hike across the galaxy to join the Andromeda strain. Anyone finding a lost Floater, hope the Pulstar hears these options. Would be impossible to spot.

On the happier side, now called Twister Pulstar Rain- bow reports a whirlwind of a ride inside a midwestern USA tornado. Twister renamed from Archibald after the exciting trip. Twister said the wrapps held and no damage occurred.

Not so lucky was another burned to a crisp Pulstar—like a marshmallow too near the campfire—named Linnette Pulstar Rainbow. Volcanoes can spit unexpectedly. Linnette made herway to the museum for a successful sparkling into a new body.

Look for performers in various joynts. Schedules avail- able.Recreational and entertainment opportunities abound. Consult listings.

As I flew quite near the voussoir entry to Neahkahnie Mountain, I decided to visit that Super-Rainbow resort at some point. But now I was too eager to radrod. Create my pattern. I reviewed my location data on my way.

I volplaned to the lower mountains near the Pacific Ocean and landed in a rehabilitated Douglas fir forest in the Tillamook Burn inside the Tillamook State Forest, a managed second growth forest. People and Pulstars are trying to rejuvenate new growth after devastating fires in six-year intervals or jinxes: 1933, 1939, 1945, 1951. The forest was handmade by school children, recreationists, politicians, foresters and timber workers working together to bring life back to around 355,000 acres with 72 million seedlings. Plants and animals returned home to 568 square miles in the Tillamook State Forest. I've got lots of ground to cover with lightening points.

Pulstars are going to try to help vitalize the firs. No longer a silver snag forest, some want to log it. We will lightening point the protected forest. Beaver, elk, deer and rabbits returned. We were warned to let wildlife remain wild. I'd sure like to get a glimpse of them however,

Finally I could radrod! I began pogoing my pattern. I love the leaps. I enjoy wrapping around mostly Douglas firs and tying the energy in lightening points.

I like knotting along the Trask and Wilson rivers. This first life is wonderful with beautiful surroundings. I'd get so absorbed I had to put on autopilot to avoid collisions. As I plopped about automatically, I could observe my surroundings.

The awesome protected soils, streams, recreational opportunities and wildlife habitat. Oh my, elk! So graceful! So elegant! This is a marvelous assignment. What a way to start my rotation! I follow hiking trails with lush undergrowth. The trails guide me away from bonking trees. The wider forest roads provide access for many species.

In the streams I might spot a fish fishers might not see. Check follows the flow while I peer at the aquatic ones. They appear startled to see me.

My quilt pattern is more crazy quilt for I have to deal with the standing people as Native American call trees. I ponder the burning of billions of board feet of prime timber with no help from fog or rain. Nature socked dry tinderbox conditions. And the repeat of the burns. Burning around snags to the soil. Plumes of smoke up to 40,000 feet.

I tune into a few tunes on the Pulse as I work. We even get some people pop channels (neat rhythms for poking the pattern) as well as western (give it a try as I'm in the West), classical, jazz, and other styles. But I love Rainbow and Super variations. Supers claim people stole many of their melodies. Rainbows learned from both groups.

I like to see the campgrounds with the tents and mobile motor homes. I did see some horses in a corral—quite impressive— but I still put the elk as most magnificent, so far.

I will have to leave this rotation soon. Axel in the Rainbow Redoubt has Flock for Fun tours on mechanical ravens. I should pulse him to suggest a tour here.

Sometimes I shrinkwrapp for some down time. I plunk my point. I am a lightening rod. I can't feel the flow through me, but the lightening point glows on our wave length. My lightening point. My mini-moon. My sunny stamp. From light or darkness light petals from my flat round bottom. I energize the roots and ground of this marvelous planet. 306 degree vision lets me take in my surroundings.

We don't require sleep to re-energize our bodies. We are fueled by our energy sources. Newness entrances me. My sense of duty and mission sustain me. Targeting my lightening points in the wilder areas requires precision and some tricky maneuvers. My body might be rigid, but my wrapps mobility is phenomenal. I romp through branches and wildflowers.

When winter comes to moister climates, many Rainbows may take down time rather than deal with snow detection. I hope there are no forest fires, so I hope for rain in these hot spots. Pulstars are to remain airborne in such areas. I've watched Hawaiian volcanoes on the Pulse. Some fireworks. I'm glad I am heading for the ocean.

We can get out of the way of floods and fires. We need to be vigilant to do so. Wrapps shelter us from heavy rain (a real asset in Oregon), hail, sleet and snow. The daily and seasonal cycles regulate weather changes and degrees of light. Such a fascinating planet!

When it's blustery, I sometimes want to sit out the storm in a crevice or near a rock rather than toss out of control on wind currents. When I am near ground I find cutting close to the edges and rounds very exciting. I like looking close at things, yet feel protected.

The animals try to get away from people. People are too numerous for Rainbows to influence. We will concentrate on Earth harmonies that feed and sustain them.

I'm kind of disappointed we can't interact with them. They'll have to be stewards of themselves. Hope some Supernals, their angels, can infiltrate them with harmony. We protect them from themselves. I just don't understand people. Can't worry too much about world wounds or I'd get muddled.

But this planet! This is the most beautiful choice I can imagine. I'm a dipstick for light. I hippity-hop like the wild rabbits. Any body that orbits a planet is a satelite. I hope someday I can finish my Quad 4 rotation and make a hover around the whole Earth.

I learned to step off my pedestal from the techniques of plastic cowboys, Indians and soldiers. They use the platforms to quilt, but just occasionally like to motate unsaddled with the foot noose.

When I take a break, I check the archives of the chess collection at Maryhill Museum in Washington to learn more about the chess sets without moves there. I'm an ivory queen that can move any direction I please. I'm off the board. I think

I am elephant ivory which bleaches white with age. Under magnification the tusk seems to radiate outward from the center.

Once ivory was inexpensive (cheap) and plentiful. Ivory was easy for people to work. Ivory was carved, pieced, turned on a lathe. Ivory accepts stains and paints. Maybe my tannish facade is from stains? Ivory is durable (great for lightening points) and holds up after extensive use (definitely a plus). Ivory will be great for radrodding.

Rainbows were once all pawns in a people game. We make our own rules and moves now. We fill out our form and record our existence.

I'm a ground-grubber, but a high-flier. As I wend away from the forest toward the sea, I know I will return to the fascination of the forest. My first life will be wonderful.

5

V-Engine in Viable Venue

The Oregon coast has public access for all, so that means me. I like the inland slant of the trees, the blowhole at Cape Perpetua, the craggy rocks, Haystack Rock near Cannon Beach, the foam on the sand, sand—wet or dry, driftwood, sea lions and whales. I don't radrod water, but I can surf on it and tumble in the waves away from people. I like the way the waves curl.

Many places don't have people roaming about. I cruise the coast light-dotting the strand, headlands and some inland places.

On the Pulse Musard in Solara sometimes gives the news in cinquos. This one was in honor of a re-sparkled Pulstar. Baseball is another life game like chess with several players and rules. In my limbless state I would never get up to bat.

Take Me Away from the Ballgame

Swat
with a bat,
smithereens
for slow Pulstar
ball.

Baseball would be a Fool's Mate game for me. Some people play chess blindfolded. I need to keep a look-see at all times in this life-game. I'm part of the Rainbow game.

I retuned in to Pulstar broadcasters Spiggott and Spandrel (Spig and Span) in Solara. Pulsations included:

Pulstar dunked in mudpot in Yellowstone made hasty exit.

Pulstar sucked in undertow off South Africa feared lost at sea. Life-spark may show up for sparkling at some point.

Pulstar blasted by bomb in a war zone. Another Pulstar triggered land mine. Stay clear of war areas. Postpone light-quilting there until hostilities cease.

Pulstar buried in avalanche in Swiss Alps. Pulstars must pay attention to their surroundings.

But most bulletins are about the successes of the radrods, the progress of the light-quilt, cooperation with Supers, opportunities for down time, new discoveries, and any insights from In2it conveyed by Pulstar assistants Shebang and Shergotty.

There are new quilt patterns to try, sharing of field experiences, entertainments: music, plays, readings of stories and poems. I try to internalize the images and sounds. Some are beautiful and some disturbing. Glad we don't have the no pain no gain philosophy. Thought pain is enough without physical pain.

As an ivory chess piece I am not as well-rounded as the energy efficient orbs on LightHome. Gravitation tends to ball things up. I feel some resistance.

As I hole up in a piece of beached driftwood, some blackened by campfires, I remember I must not entomb and to have a getaway from holes. Weather and people can impede progress. I don't mind being my own ivory tower. In my secluded haunts I can review the archives and enjoy the Pulse. I am ivory towered from the world and some realities. I'm in uncharted, unenlightened places for Pulstars.

Sometimes I just have to make my move and deal with the consequences.

But mostly I'm a verb, bobbling, bopping about. It's nice to be material not immaterial. I'm a material witness! Quite fun being buffeted by wind, but I can't steer myself well. The beach side cabins, homes, hotels stare at the sea.

I saw a few beach walkers with the bump packs. No. Check the archives for bunches on backs. "Check your back," it says. Yes. backpacks. Another term when on the beach, beachcombers. Lots of beach terms.

This sea duty is as pleasant as the forest. Not really on any special time, just keep poking away at the pattern I downloaded. Have to make modifications sometimes, but the little pricks of light can't be seen from very faraway. But the coastline is sprinkled with my lightening points and looking good.

When radrodding, I'm winging it. V is wings. I'm a v-particle in vestments. Floating on the sea breeze like a kite.

So much to learn. A miracle a minute. Earth is the place to play games. More than sports, table games and good vs evil. I'm glad I'm a chess queen to play any game I encounter. I'm full of opening moves and tricks. I know the first moves can put you in a weak or strong position for the rest of the game. Hope not to have to fork, skewer or pin.

I want to stomp my stamp, keep darkness in check. I don't want to be a Fool's mate. I want to begin my checkered life boldly and not be kept in check. Time to be queen not pawn. Light is right on the chess board. The king's surrender is not my aim for this game. I Way-V Pulstar Rainbow number 753335 pledge to make my medallions of light as intensely as possible.

I will try to remember In2it's instructions from our travel across space:

1. Avoid fires of all kinds.
2. Steer clear of people.
3. Stay outside most buildings.
4. Visit harmonious homes for shelter.
5. Do your duties lightfully.

6. Prepare for heavy weather.
7. Live joyfully.

Check is my invisible energy screen, my vehicle for transportation, instruction, protection, shelter—my van. Shrinkwrapp will delay aging. Old ivory is shielded from the elements. I will keep my energy source in wraps. We are static-celled not changing-celled or mutating. We are not watery, but pretty arid in construction. Some of the Pulstars are more flexible than others. We seek our own meaning and purpose in life. I am thinking about my rippler time.

I have entered form, activated my life, serve my radrod purpose and will do so enthusiastically until called to another mission in another form in another place. I want to be a powerful jolt to the Earth's energy grid.

Kalahari Proverb I found on the Pulse says things are powerful in proportion to their smallness. The small thing gives meaning to the great. There are big ideas in small things.

I intend to plunk and plug into the planet. I just have so much light within I just want to shine. Time to mobilize my molecules. I want to make a solid impression. I tack my point and move on according to design, prodded by pattern.

I'm en passant. I'm off to Neahkahnie Mountain where Jettison pulsed he is reading some of his poetry at the Super-Rainbow resort. Hope he's improved. Maybe Onterra and Albedo will stop by. I hover over beach breaks. The beach grass seems to wave me onward.

6

Valid Vacation

Time seems to run timelessly in the wild and by the sea. I was not sure how long it had been since I saw my cluster of friends. En route to the joynt, I was tugged to the rides at Seaside and whizzed through the shops at Cannon Beach. I did not interact with people, just observed them in their pursuits by the sea. I avoided them on the beach as they avoided undertows.

I set my sights on Neahkahnie Mountain, the legendary contact place for the alignment of the portals to contact LightHome through the huge crystal. It was the Supernaturals' favorite getaway. Neahkahnie is a larger, Super-sized version of the mound.

Rainbows visit more frequently now since their alliance. A new entrance to a large entertainment area welcomes all-comers. Neahkahnie Mountain is one of the shielded areas. Supers placed protective shields over Solara, the Rainbow Museum and the Rainbow Redoubt as well. People can't detect what is inside the cave or mountain. No fear of detection here. But I keep my energy shield around me.

I am about to be a vacationer in a vacationland joynt. Maybe I'll get some ideas what to do with my down time except listen to the Pulse.

Neahkahnie Mountain is near Oswald West State Park, Neahkahnie Beach and Manzanita on Oregon Coast Highway 101. I flew with the seagulls. The rainbow arch entrance invited me inside.

There are many small theaters (without chairs). I do not sit anyway. Supers and Rainbows jockey for position in the air. Those that prefer to sit usually sit in front or under the winged ones or those in flight.

31

I pulsed Jettison to see where he might be. He was still in transit, but would meet me soon in the Pulstar hangout, Pulsation Station. Various alcoves had lighting, but the main route was not glamoured by Supers or light-painted by Rainbows. Neon-like signs arced over entrances to the various entertainment and discussion areas.

Wings whirred. Words buzzed. Music beat. The service crew had Radrod and Rippler gathering places. The creative expression and passion types of scientists and artists gathered to share their quzests. Some broke our tasks down to Lighteners: Radrods in service, enlighteners; special individual pursuits for the good of the whole, and considered lightening points to be metaphorical. All these word games and word plays. I did not come for discussion, but for entertainment.

I could not help but overhear the Pulstar cosmic energy engineers complaining and criticizing. Some want reassignment to other areas on Earth or in the cosmos. Golly there are microgalaxies too! The Pulstar Planners Shebang and Shergotty could get more dissonance than they planned for.

Some Pulstars did not attempt to modulate harmonic vibrations. Some doubted they could save Earth for the well-being of all. Some upstarts wanted to jumpstart independence movements to takeover Earth in service to themselves. I thought only harmonizing life-sparks would come. The Cosmic Pinata left the loophole of free will.

Will this New Wave evolve to be more harmonic? Supers and most Rainbows have. Some Earthlings haven't. Hopefully all life forces will commit to Earth and all its inhabitants. These drop-outs worry me. I learned over the Pulse that only 974,736 Pulstars arrived. That is fewer dropouts lost to other cosmic causes than we predicted.

Radrods go off duty for short or long periods to follow their Rippler inclinations. Some are Ripplers full-time, serving and expressing their talents to help the whole.

Do we need maintenance engineers to see if lightening points leak and find Pulstars who can't sprout light?

I heard some Rainbow songs spilling passion, pain, protest and praise into the corridors. Groups called Pulsion and Fusion. Heard part of a Pulstar group called the Pulsators.

The New Wave want to be on the airwaves and in the joynts spreading their message. They want to express themselves as Ripplers, not just Radrods. New selves in old forms. The First Wave planners and commentators now have company.

The Pulse said that people-girls learn how to be women from other women, not from their dolls. But we give them practice. This chess queen plans to be a Pulstar-Rainbow learning from the Rainbow Path of those who walked it before me. I like the light quilt designs and weeds. It will take courage and there will be obstacles. I have a naive strength, daring and derring-do. Where will the new wave Pinata Pulse go? How many other bursts we are not aware of? I shrinkwrapped as I meandered the hallways.

Onterra and Albedo could not get away to hear Jettison's first poetry reading. As I waited for Jettison I doodled v's on a wall: sideways facing each other like noses in conversation. Upwards was my beloved mountains above a normally positioned v for valley. I added outward pointing side pieces converting them into petals for a flower. I attached four v's pointing outward in the four directions with a dot in a center to make my own floral design. I attached five outward pointing v's to make a star. Light-paint made my images glow golden.

I was still doodling when Jettison found me. He dashed to the staging area. Not a prompt poet. Or especially polite considering I did go out of my way to attend the reading and he arrived just moments before show time.

Jettison spruced up for the reading, daubing light-paint on his hat (now green) and his pedestal (now deep brown). When it came time to read he levitated a bit and in a very strong voice projected two poems. I had not paid attention to the other poets in the reading as I was busy doodling and musing about the state of Pulstar affairs. I did listen to Jetti-son. I hoped for his best.

Calling to the Moon

April new moon
makes me wow-swoon
marble balloon
watching.

Howling out loud
in Rainbow crowd.
Grey-white thin cloud
swiftly swatching.

Maybe it is April? Must be some weird form he picked up from Sylvianne. Wish it had a v-word. V's open things up.

A Cosmic Trip

We came across the universe at least the speed of light
    to spark an older planet.
Our brand-new life-sparks ignite former Earthen forms
    to jumpstart a life-infusion.
We are the pin in the pinata—pin at a—linchpin
    for a life starting with A.
We are new notes for the harmonic sound to play back
    to music of the spheres.

We are immortal, but our life span here is uncertain
    for we might leap elsewhere.
We are free formers, free performers, free reformers,
    free transformers, free to be.
We chose to come to hue the rainbow, nourish all life,
    pulse energy, light the path.
We leap spot to spot, life to life, light to light,
    thought to thought with firm commitment.

Pulstars pulse with stellular brilliance and beat
the drum of a darkened planet.

Well, a bit polemic, but I encouraged him and assured him that his internship with Sylvianne had improved his style.

Other Pulstar poets who called themselves part of a Starpole Cluster droned on for it seemed eons. Jettison and I took a break to talk and returned to hear a poet calling himself Rip Von Wrinkle. He was mending the rips and ironing the ripples in his poems.

Jettison and I could not chat long. Our cluster had time in the cosmos for conversation. We are busy in a world. Jettison was off to another internship in poetry with Wings coordinator Maraki Shiri. He gets to travel with the song, dance and pageant troop to learn various approaches to poems. Should be fun.

I don't have time to hang around a joynt. I plan to be punctual for my next assignment. My next orientation is in Summit, Oregon, for rural rotations.

Both of us are happy with our choices so far. As I drift to Summit, I recall the sounds and sights at Neahkahnie. I can see where Pulstars could be drawn to the energy and rhythm of the light-blasting joynts.

7

Vulnerable Vestiges

As I headed for Summit I took a southern dip detour to the Presidents' Grove near Oakridge and Westfir where the old growth Douglas fir stand tall. How I love the tall trees! But I love these trees best of all. These protected leftovers from the manic logger times which downed most of them. How could illegal loggers cut old growth when so many legal loggers took so many? Old growth oozes the sap of survival, stalwardness, wisdom and weathering the ages. Yes, I need to remember the light-stitches are farther apart in the wilderness. Incredible energy here.

I meditate in this presence of greatness. I try to design my interior. I want to light-paint art, load my archives, listen to Pulse, my muse, communicate. I've observed turbulent and tranquil clouds. I shelter from and hover in weather. I will find down spots, former Rainbow hostels and hear the Rainbow stories.Maybe the universe is a variety of life games on different playing fields. Different rules. Different power plays. Different challenges than good and evil choices.

What else should I care about? I worry about the struggle against destruction and disease on the planet. On the Pulse they talked about Bracken Cave in Texas. We are not bothered by the ammonia from droppings of millions of freetail bats. They eat insects and are dangerous if sick. Am I here to enlighten bats? Or are the scientists in Solara studying their night flight skills? I did not listen to why we were interested in them. I had switched channels.

I am a wild thing in the wilderness of a first life. Space was unfathomable to comprehend, but Earth is still stupendous to me. To be so small and required to do such a big task can feel overwhelming sometimes. Some grasses are taller than I am. I'm definitely at the grassroots level.

To make a lightening point I parachute into underbrush, scamper by my zip-drive under low branches, stop on a stone. I confront rough terrain. I dive into the colors of meadows and wildflowers. I've experienced the thrill of riding the rapids, the float on a calm pond. I've docked at lilypad islands or looked upward from flat rocks. I've surfed the ocean waves without bursting my bubble.

In the wilderness the Supers of the fairy variety still romp in the water and branches. Supers like their privacy so we have to remember they can see us.

In the Cascades past volcanic eruptions from Mazama, Mt. St. Helens sculpted the landscape. Views of Crater Lake with Wizard Island are spectacular.

Pulstars are doing a lot of double-dipping in the Pacific Northwest. Some are checking to see if the initial radrod work held. It seems that the lightening points are holding. This area was popular with the first Radrods.

I'm not cosmic royalty. My queenly crown brushes air. The queen was invented to make chess a more exciting game. I hope I am here to make a more exciting life.

I'm a down to earth Earthen making moves to save us all. Once bodiless, I am a lump without limbs. Pulstars are the light-switches to bring light to a dark universe.

I'm having some difficulty making my Waves in English. What a weird language! Can't sound it out a lot of the time. So I guess. Seems notating music would be easier. If I add lyrics I'd have to spellcheck. I attach words to my notes and carry them in my thoughts more than expressing words on a surface or telepathically. Eventually I'll download onto a CD.

This is my first life. I'll savor it as long as I can. There are no lifetime guarantees. I'll speculate options and remain open to new opportunities.

Soon I will conjure and cast my bauble for take off. I look forward to light-stamping my round bottom in a new place.

The infintessimal and invisible can be heavy in some scale. Yes, wide bottoms and ivory make excellent conductors to connect energy. Maybe I'm an empty peace pipe letting harmonious energies flow through me. Need to make waves wherever we are sent.

Before I headed north to Summit, I light-sculpted a solitary rainbow-swirled overlayed white candle on one branch in tribute to the old growth from a newcomer. Other Rainbows can leave tapered candles to flicker on this tree of light and other favorite trees. Hopefully other Pulstars and people will come by and pay their respects. We live in coinciding, concurrent, hopefully congruous realities. I hope if people leave candles—they don't light them and burn down the forest.

Autopilot Summit. No detours. I am a punctual Pulstar.

II.

Orange: Dawn

Rural Hayseeds

Light Places: Musard Rippler Rainbow

Light
can shine
the brightest
in the darkest
place.

Light
can glow
where things grow—
caged or open
fields.

Smog,
fog, clouds
conceal stars.
Hope the weather
clears.

8

A V Sprouts
A V Grows

Near villages and small towns with names such as Deadwood, Burnt Woods, Chitwood, on a pass in the Coast Range is the community of Summit. Happy Hollow Road leads into the winding Summit highway. I followed the road into town.

About fifty Pulstars camped out in a field near an abandoned farmhouse and barn. The silvered boards reminded me of the snags in the Tillamook forest.

I knew Jettison was on the fly with Wings. Albedo pulsed his regrets from Findhorn in Scotland. So I was delighted to see Onterra and Hugh would do the orientation.

Onterra and I found an upright fence post and caught up on news. We pulsed each other from time to time, but gaps of time were filled. Hugh wanted a Pulstar planner to help with surface operations. Pulstars now outnumbered the remaining Rainbows. Though we all called ourselves Rainbows, Pulstar was the middle name for most who popped from the pinata.

Onterra and Hugh planned to travel globally with the orientations. They were also training other Pulstars to help with orientations and go to Solara to help find solutions to any glitches Rainbows encountered on their rounds. Some problems of scheduling, overlapping quilting, unpopular quilt patterns, turf tussles with Supers, power failures, static from the Pulse, emergency services need more Pulstar participants... and the list went on. Solara is the Super-Rainbow headquarters. Overall planners Karen and Jorden and the Super-Rainbow Council are there. New plans to include Pulstars in planning positions and other areas were a priority.

Onterra did not mind caves like Solara, but she was planning surface operations. She would spend most of her time on top of the landscape. Onterra knew Hugh missed his previous partner Osmunda who preferred to be a dancer. Onterra just wanted to do the job and be his friend. She has an upbeat quality and independent spirit.

I noticed Hugh called her On. He called his former co-planner Osmunda, Oz. She would rather dance with Wings. He has a thing about nicknames. Calls his first partner Karen, Hub. She founded the First Rainbow Liberation Movement. In various tones I hear Hugh say, "Come on, On." Not all tones are harmonious. Probably the reason he is on his third partner.

Onterra pulsed the following rules to the Pulstar Hayseeds as they called themselves for this rotation.

Ground Rules for Rural Areas

1. Don't drop into dung. Don't get under foot, hoof, paw, wheels.
2. Beware of machines of all kinds. You are protected with invisibility, but not from destruction.
3. Don't become like a needle in a haystack.
4. Focus energies and light for plant growth and animal comfort.
5. Don't ride livestock—especially tails.
6. Be careful near water or fire.
7. Sustain and maintain your energies. Energies can be focused and harnessed for many purposes.

Hugh then gave an impassioned speech saying, "Don't become poppets! Keep out of people's hands. Avoid messy, sticky matters. Linger longer in organic gardens and see how growth occurs naturally. Pay attention to water changes and levels. Avoid corrosives.

Be aware and never allow yourself to be used as a poppet, those dolls representing people used for magic.

Anything done to the doll was supposed to be done to someone. The poppets contained bits and pieces from the target. We do not want to be used to harm or control anyone. Some poppets were also sacrifices. Made from sheaves of the previous harvest, they were burned or drowned to return nourishment to the earth. English and Welsh harvest festivals involved destroying the cornbaby or Kernababy. We are not surrogate sacrifices.

We help sustain nature in other ways and need to keep our bodies whole to do our work. You are an independent agent on the Rainbow team. Go freely and lightly."

We practiced radrodding in the tall grass, sliding down the gaping barn roof, walked the wires of the fences, balanced so we could aim our light. We hovered like bees over the flowers and weeds. We don't discriminate against weeds. Then we huddled like honeycomb to camp. We'd shrinkwrapp to dance or inflate our wrapps to tent for discussions.

Fairies still lived in some fields. They tended to prefer suburban gardens. So many left for their own planet Superior. Many waited in their other world, Avalon. The Pacific Northwest still had troops in the Cascades. But in Oregon, more locally, they tended to work in organic farms and gardens. We were warned Supers were somewhat territorial and did not relish intrusions. In this area there were several organic farming operations. Some were communities that worked cooperatively. The pesticides that were a problem for Supers before their Slips, were no longer a problem. The problem was there were too few Supers to cover all the areas they formerly covered. Part of the planning for Hugh and Onterra and the computerized data collectors in Solara was detecting where the Supers were living. Most of the fairies went suburban because of chemical complications only to find chemical enhancement in many of those gardens.

Wild animals are more accustomed to Supers and they co-exist peacefully. Farm livestock are another matter. Livestock have interacted with people. Sometimes not kindly.

Supers passed on the suggestion not to pester livestock or get whacked off by their tails. Rainbows can soothe livestock with mendbeam, our healing powers and play music around them.

Plants, however, are a Super specialty. Supers passed on tips how we could help plants flourish. Supers also have a close relationship with trees. Like birds they like to make rest stops on their limbs, and sometimes fairies nest there.

People and animals benefit as we sustain beauty and food harvests. All life forces can work to sustain the livability of the planet. Rainbows do not view plants and animals as products.

We don't grow physically. With people gender depends on where the bumps are and who gestates and delivers children. We are often pre-adolescent models and don't produce offspring. But we can help with Earthlings feeding needs. We help the plants and livestock to grow to sustain people.

Soon it was time to say farewell to Hugh and Onterra. I was off to some viable, working farms in the area. It was time to begin my radrodding. I dropped my point into vegetable crops, grass seed fields, a few orchards. I try to aim my mark accurately, but sometimes in orchards the roots trip me up. It is time for the cultivated land. I would encounter pesticides and other products introduced into crops and creatures.

When I met my first horse up close, I was fascinated. The horse did not share my fascination. He took me for some variety of flea or fly and whacked the swift tail at me. Fortunately I was quick and dodged the swat.

Cows seems more interesting in munching than moving. I perched on the back of one slowly mooving creature to take in some rays and the bovine never acknowledged my presence.

Now pigs were in rather mucky areas as a whole. I did not touch ground, but hovered just above the mud to make my lightening point. Trying to place a point in the midst of chickens is a tricky feat. I liked the non-interference policy with wild animals. Can't avoid some contact with animals in rural areas.

Can't avoid farm machinery either. Roving under farm equipment to make a light point makes me wonder when the mechanical monster might move and how quickly. Some times I wish I had a companion for a lookout. 360 degree vision is sometimes just not enough. Sometimes Pulstars pair up and cluster into companies for companionship, meeting at a designated spot.

Still not much contact with people, which is probably best. I saw some people in a community commune near Dead-wood. They know how to validate valetudarians.

I'm radiant energy traveling as a wave motion, the en-ergy of electromagnetic waves and more. Energy is all around us. Some focused. Some contained. So many mystical and mysterious energies we know so little about.

Guess I am not the aggie type. I can't smell the smells, feel the hairs and feathers and other skin coverings, taste the foods the farms produce. Agriculture is to feed Earthlings. I don't need to feed. Plants and animals don't appeal to me in an edible way.

Maybe I'm more a mountaineering type. A tower type. I wish I could skip the rest of the rural and suburban rotations and go straight to the mountains and skyscrapers.

But I will have to leave the hills and rills, for vineyards in the valley, then over the mountains to irrigated fields. Vast ranches and farms require many Pulstars. I'll just tune in the Pulse on my way.

9

Vernaling the Vernacular

The Willamette Valley has a string of vineyards. They are pleasant places with orderly growth, supportive of vines for wine. Since I don't eat or drink, I view them in somewhat different context. I'm not here to entwine the vines, but to rejuvenate them into exquisite grapes...for others' consumption.

On the Pulse I learned there are over 130 vineyards in Oregon. One has an observation tower that looks over the Willamette Valley—a mini-mountain I must check out. Many vineyards have lakes with swans and ducks, bridges, lovely landscapes, some surrounded by forest. They seek sunlight and cool nights to grow grapes. They store the wine in big barrels. Pinot Noir seems to grow here especially well.

They don't just make wine from grapes, but other fruits such as peach, currants, cherry, boysenberry, blueberry, blackberry, huckleberry, loganberry, raspberry and other combinations. Since I do not drink, I just enjoy the views and festivities.

At the wineries people gather for weddings, celebrations, festivals, music and entertainment, buffets and dinners, tasting booths. They swirl the wine in the glass to nose—smell the fragrance which I can't. Some people stomp grapes in big tubs with their feet. I prefer to stomp lightening points.

Various vehicles drive down the rows. I like a horse and carriage (but keep my distance). I stamp my pattern amid the acreage and trellises. Trellises hold the grapes toward the sunlight. Vines can be trained up and down.

I tune in music or news from the Pulse. Some snippets from Kisam from the Rainbow Redoubt on the Pulse.

Axel has openings for a Flock for Fun Tour to the glaciers of Greenland. Pulse Axel at the Rainbow Museum for reservations.

Advice from a Pulstar trapped for awhile in a bank vault, remember to keep doors open.

Pulstars Spiggott and Spandrel have finished their communications rotations to the various Rainbow broadcast locations. Spig and Span will be broadcasting from Solara.

With no orientation to vineyards, I was left alone. Have to rely on my hayseed knowledge for the rest of my rural rotation. I'm not about to whine on the vine. It is beautiful in the vineyard. Still I yearn for the higher places.

I saw my time here was short because of the needs of Central and Eastern Oregon agricultural operations. I hoped I get some uncultivated areas with tumbleweed.

But to be honest, this really is a Breathers' place. Breathers need to preserve the air and reduce the Greenhouse Effect so the crops will grow. They need water to drink and land to feed them. We do not need wine of the vineyards or anything to eat or drink or breathe. We just need enough gravity to stay attached to the planet.

Small is better for our work. Most larger editions of Rainbows are sparkled smaller to get them off the shelf and away from captivity. They were like corked wine bottles.

The process of Sparkling is reassuring. When a Rainbow body is immobilized (in view of people) or damaged, another body can come from the museum, be placed head to head with the other body and the life-spark leaps into the now animated, free-to-go body. If my chess-queenly form can't play the game, I will get a new game piece. If this happens, I'd like a stiff with free-moving limbs. It's fun to speculate what I would be if not royalty in a democracy.

Orbs of LightHome would fit in with these grapes. My Check weaves me vine to vine as I follow the pattern. This pattern is called Hydra after the long snake-like constellation. Sometimes I check lightening points of earlier radrods in the region to see if the point holds. It does.

As I waited out a heavy drencher, so common in the valley, I received a Pulse from Jettison. He was performing his poems in Wings pageants. Currently he was in a Pulstar joynt in New Zealand. Many Rainbows consolidated to the American West before recruits from LightHome and the Cosmic Pinata came to help them redeem the Rainbow traditions.

It is great Jettison gets to travel widely. Not sure too much caving would be good for him. Most joynts are underground however. He is learning how to compose poems in Global, English (his home base language) and try to translate into other local languages while on tour. He thinks it might take awhile to get the knack of this. He thinks Global is the best for Rainbow and Super audiences.

Traveling can enrich a poet. This is good for a poet without much of a life yet. He could have been stuck in the underground of Solara. He just might get better.

The rain let up so I returned to radrodding. Oregon has many boggy, soggy, wet places. Water is so fascinating. No wonder Earthlings want to gulp it inside. Seems to oil their internal engines. I like to take down time on the banks of or on the riverteeth of the Willamette River. I can not feel the splash, but I can experience being engulfed by foam or drifting on waves. I like to look at fish.

I found a people-written poem about this river tucked in our archives by a Rainbow Radiant.

American Heritage River

Once osprey, waterfowl, salmon, fish thrived here;
oaks, maples, forests, floods, fisher, marten, banks.
Swamps, chest-high grass, nature could change the stream
    course.
Deer, bear, elk, fish, fir, oaks, Kalapooya leave.

Hogs rooted starchy bulbs. Camas prairie goes.
Snags, drift-piles, debris, jams, river channels go.
Off-channel aquatic zones, revetments bind.
Dredge, mine, farm, irrigate, angle flow and shore.

Paved, plowed, drained, diked, dammed, fenced,
    herbicided flow.
Farm, urban run-off, pulp, furans, sewage spoil.
Spilled toxins, waste discharge, contaminants bring
us deformed fish, osprey nests in power poles.

Fish, wildlife, aquatic organisms—us—
we need health, planning, laws, river's return. Hope
can restore a river. Connect Willamette.
We treat your water to drink, swim, fish, boat, live.

Heal again. Leave murky, dirty, algaed past.
Cleanse. Restore riverteeth. Scour our valley clean.
Swim salmon in rescued riparian zones.
Fly osprey over a river that runs freed.

Oregonians have worked to clean up their acts. Must always be vigilant. Unfortunately Rainbows can't do their tasks.

Another downpour in the Oregon tradition. I tuned into the archives for some Helpful Hints about Oregon from the Pulse: Spig reporting.

Field burning in the valley leaves burned fields which seen from air blacken and flatten green and appear asphalt parking lots. Grass seeds growers create smoke which Pulstars avoid.

Many people in Oregon have such dewy faces moistened by dampness, unwrinkled, clear and young. We just look wet. Slugs do seem to hold conventions in muddy yards. They drown in beer or crinkle in a sprinkle of salt. Be kind to these gooey creatures.

Forest screen clearcuts, provide playgrounds for wild
life or hiding for Big Foot. Forests are great getaways
for Pulstars.

Bottles on the roadsides are retrieved and recycled in
plastic bags. Some bottles blasted on beach rocks.
Pulstars steer away from sharp edges and empties.

Reclusive writers and artists commune with nature with
computers. Remember to record your journeys for the
archives and for Rainbow Chronicles.

I tuned out further comments. I wanted to just take a
break and make my notations. All this frenetic hopping about
gets boring. I begin to think of visiting a joynt soon. But I
don't see time for that until near the end of the hayseed rota-
tion.

It is taking me some time to get the knack of the vine-
yards between McMinnville and Eugene area. I wish I'd en-
counter other Pulstars, vainglorious vagrants in the vines of
the vineyard.

10

Vantages and Vistas

As I left valley entanglements behind, I flew inside Check into the Cascades. Wow! Mt. Jefferson, Three-Fingered Jack, The Three Sisters, Black Butte— beautiful. I recalled my fondness for Douglas firs. Soon I was in the town of Sisters.

I strolled through a quilt show in the touristy, resort town of Sisters. Quilts attached to buildings and rails buckled in the wind. Sign said they do this the second Saturday in July.

I tried to find some new ideas for my light quilt patterns. It was hot with a forest fire in the distance. Abundant water tanks. I rested on one to watch the crowds admiring the dazzling designs and colors of the quilts. Some even had rainbows in their quilts. Unaffected by the heat or heights of the crowds, I had a clear view of the carefully pieced and cleverly designed quilts. I had to pay attention to how close to the quilt and to people I was. Navigating around ever-moving people can be a challenge. I usually just hover a few feet above them.

The llamas in the area, like sheep, are my favorite animals. I played a little music for the startled llamas. They can't see us apparently, so it would be confusing.

Nearby Bend has many resorts, is near skiing areas and has recreational activities on the Deschutes River. Early Rainbows have lightpointed these areas so I will get to roll with the tumbleweeds as I continue East to large irrigated ranches and less populated areas.

I tuned into the Pulse as I watched the arid landscape pass beneath me. The network of Pulstar broadcasters operate channels called Pulstations. Pulstars have a lot to learn before they twinkle in the arts. We are working on images in poetry and art and sounds in writing and music. I kind of like playing around with light configurations.

No matter how how mundane, I turn into Pulstations often to relieve the monotony of radrodding. If I follow the pattern on autopilot, I am free to ripple, do my own expressions. A sample of some Span comments:

Pulstars rescued geese whose mouths were glued from eating slugs.

Pulstar tripped in a worm hole much to the annoyance of the worm. Worms do not want our intervention.

Be grateful you can't smell. Pulstars don't have an odor. Flowers' fragrance is supposed to be quite compelling, however. But since you can't smell, concentrate on what you can do like light-projection and magnetism. You can energize to ignite light and sound. You also help the blossoming of flowers so others can smell them.

I am trying to find my balance between radrod and ripple time. I like to be in the audience at a joynt rather than as a performer, I think. I need to sample more joynts to get a better sense of the places. It is different viewing them on Pulse and being there.

There are debates about division of Radrod and Rippler time. Time in service to the planet and time in service to the individual and Rainbow causes. They are gathering data on Rainbows' choices. If too many choose to be a Rippler too much of the time, this planet's light-quilt will never get finished.

Meanwhile, I'm on the range. This is beef country. I console the cattle with concerts as I radrod between them and their hooves. This is like a rodeo I heard about.

Rural domesticated animals seem to have a different fate than domesticated pets. People prefer to have different relationships with different animals which seems to effect their eatability.

I like wide open spaces. Sometimes I feel like the Vedic god Varuna responsible for the natural and moral order of the cosmos. But mostly I am a vaquero. A herder and cowqueen.

I knew to stay away from horses. A mane might be a better choice than a tail to ride. Less chance to be flicked off? The horse did not like a tail rider no matter how light I was. I was heavier than a fly or flea, but a horse isn't fond of any of us. I did not repeat that performance for an encore.

My career as a rough rider never really began. It could end my Radrod choice. I narrowly escaped agitated hooves. I'm no buckaroo.

I could not imagine the vast vistas on Earth any more than I could imagine the immenseness of space. In Eastern Oregon my vision revealed distant horizons. I connected my patterns in the open spaces. I worked many of the places not experiencing too much intervention.

On down time I explored the lava formations and tubes, the volcanic eruptions' reddish debris. Climbing Smith Rocks following the moves of people climbers. Watching the recreationists on Deschutes River. Never seemed to see any other Pulstars around. I did not take time to explore any of the Rainbow hostels, rehabs and joynts in the lava tubes. I wanted to see as much of the surface as I could before I moved on.

Although all places have their appeal, I yearn for the mountains. On down time I looked at some images of the South American Andes. I dream of Aconcagua in Argentina.

I dotted along irrigation ditches. Boring in contrast to rushing rivers. I visited dam-dinosaurs blocking the river to give power to the people and death to the salmon. I thought it would be fun to roll down the side of a dam—more a roll down tumbling inside Check. But I needed to consult Pulse about my next destination. On to the Palouse in Washington. Ride 'em chessqueen!

11

Viridescent Veneer

Palouse country is grain country, green until the wheat and safflower and other grains on the multi-cropped hills come to fruition. Looked at views in various growing stages on the Pulse. Headed for the Tri-Cities area. I tried not to be distracted by the city lights and taller buildings. But I did peek. Passed over where the Snake and Columbia coverged at Sacajawea State Park near Pasco. Gorgeous white and blue lighted bridges.

Looked at a few dams. Little Monumental Dam is not so massive as those on the Columbia. But did not linger. I was heading for my next rural pattern.

The reddish Snake River canyon was awesome as I headed for the Pullman area. I was going to do some radrodding around the small town of Palouse. Looks really Old West with the pioneer storefronts. Many abandoned stores. Pulse says now it is a bedroom community for Pullman.

I made a stop at the public gardens to drop a few points. I visited the home of avid gardeners who really planted their yard and had a green house. There is a Hobbit Trail lit by lights through a thicket. That was a neat flight.

But my mission was to place some lightening points in the grain fields. Machines, irrigation and rodents could get in the way of an easy shot and make a light-pattern variation. I say rodents because I don't want to zap them if they are in the way.

I worked for long hours because after one more farm rotation, I was meeting Jettison in a joynt in Bayhorse, Idaho. Palouse country is near the Idaho border in Washington.

I radrodded at Smoot Hill, Kamiak Butte and near Vantine Road. Took a gander over to South Palouse River.

I concluded that most of the wild west is tamed. The rural aspect cultivated with genetically redesigned seeds with pesticides and innoculated livestock. They have lost some of their diversity and wildness.

Frogs are endangered by polluted ponds. Fish are pen-reared. Salmon struggle up fish ladders and disturbed streams. I wonder just how much our lightening points can do to help. I'm assured by the Pulse and archives that we are enhancing the energy grid enough to impulse growth. I do not want to be a virion or a virus.

No dancing the villanella with Supers. No chatting with Rainbows in sight. I guess I am a bit lonely even with access to the Pulse.

Sometimes I ride over a truck or car and wonder about the lives of the drivers. Wish mind-reading came with our nanos.

Sometimes I fly with birds, but they really do not have much to say. They are on their way to their next destination, just as I am.

Sometimes I cruise the craggy canyons and rocky outcropping and admire their texture and beauty.

My 360 degree vision can take in the multi-colored, multi-cropped hills and plains.

The wild regions of Oregon and the rural areas of Oregon and Washington are astonishing. I know my first life is going to be a good one.

I have experienced some turbulence. I was topsy-turvy in a storm I thought I could ride out. I was bouncing in my bubbled Check. When I splashed into a wind-whipped river, I bobbled along until I figured out it might be time to take flight or take cover.

Another close call came when a dozing man on a tractor awoke before I detected. Another close call. I misjudged the height of a silo and bounced hard against the side. I was discombobulated. I was solo navigating, free flying. I should have gone on autopilot. Well, you don't expect any buildings in miles of acres of crops. When I landed I found myself rolled under a pig trough. The mud coated Check. My vision was blurred. But my bubble didn't burst. I set autopilot for the nearest waterhole and took a dunk. All's clear.

After a few misadventures in turbulence, I sought down times. I mean down time not upside down time. I needed time to harmonize and create. I experimented with light-sculpture.

Palouse country will await the verdure, veridical, verdant version of their seasonal cycle. But I want to get to my next rural rotation.

12

Vigilant Viewer

As I dawdled in midair, I knew I needed another assignment in a rural region before I could go on to the suburban orientation. Since I hope to go to see Jettison, I wanted to radrod not too far from Idaho.

My assignments are to be in Quad 4 for now. The quads are divided:

1. 90 degrees west to zero longitude.
2. Longitude zero prime meridian to 90 degrees east.
3. 90 degrees east to 180 degrees west of international dateline.
4. International dateline to 90 degrees west.

But I am limited by my intentions as well. I do not want to visit a vivarium or consort with emus and edible animals. Had a run-in with an emu which I'd like to forget. Guess I am not an animal person. Don't want a dairy farm. Probably too many chickens there also.

Maybe I can find an uncultivated rural area. People decide the animals' fate, the quality of air, land and water. People are top animal at the moment. Insects bug and infect them. Some tainted fish and flesh or poisoned vegetables get them sick. Other animals can live in the wild, caged, in a zoo, as a house pet, or raised for food. I like that we don't excrete anything.

We are energy-enhancers of electromagnetic energies. We can't do much about air and water quality. People are watery and need air, water and land to sustain them. We are independent of resources since we don't consume. Once our form is created, that's all one takes. We even recycle our bodies.

People are going to have to handle their own energies. We can't mop up all their messes. With feuds, battles, natural disasters, they need all the help they can get.

So I chose to head toward Ontario, Oregon, down to the Malheur Wildlife Refuge. Now it isn't technically rural and it isn't technically wild. But here I know life is protected and I want to know how people are doing with protected areas. I do have free will like all sentient creatures.

On my way I listened to commentary and travel tips from Betty the Birder: The Malheur in May.

To get to Malheur you experience a number of ecosystems.

When you leave the Willamette Valley you cross the Cascades filled with Douglas fir, dense undergrowth and the breathtaking snowcapped peaks.

Then you are in drier, red, crackly Ponderosa pine country. Here are deciduous forests, maples and aspen. Blue lupine and Indian paintbrush are nearby.

Twisty, gnarly, shaggy-pealing, juniper on sage-covered hills. Willows along rivers. Watch the willow's colorful leafing. Look out for mountain and western bluebirds, hawks, maybe a golden eagle or vulture.

Malheur is on the Pacific Flyway. Migratory birds love it here. It is a protected area. Other area residents: jackrabbits, nighthawks, burrowing owls, swallows, golden-eyed duck, rattlesnakes, white-headed woodpecker.

As we fly into Malheur look at the Pueblo mountains to the south. See the Steens? French Glen nestled in. Notice wetlands. Ah, May at Malheur. Hear the singing meadow lark?

See the waterbirds (like cinnamon teals, pied bill grebes and ruddy ducks with colorful mating bills) on ponds and islands. Witness the little black coots, rusty-looking shovelers, down-curved beaked, white ibis. Oh, the white pelican, larger than other water birds.

Hear the sandhill cranes. Shorebirds include the long-billed curlew and Great Blue Herons looking for frogs and fish. Might see a bittern.

Warblers in the willows. Listen to the blackbirds. Canadian geese, California quail and big-eyed owl youngsters are visible in May. Newborn birds can be different sizes. People think they hatch at different times in the same nest.

May migrants passing through are colorful orioles, lazuli buntings, gray flycatchers. Groups of birders with binoculars try to see favorite and special birds. Too many creatures to comment on them all. You just have to go to see for yourself.

Wherever I radrod or ripple, I watch for the numerous varieties of birds and their diverse habitats. Visit my bird gallery. I have images of hundreds of birds. My list increases rapidly as I am on a global tour.

Thanks for tuning in to The Malheur in May. This is Betty the Birder wishing you happy flights.

Also en route I heard a weird bulletin from Spig on the Pulstation. Some free will gets out of hand.

A Pulstar looking at an interstellar gravel display of a meteor shower decided to take off for the cosmos without the encumbrance of a body. However the Pulstar did not have any coordinates to reconnect with galactarian companions. Currently the Pulstar is a Floater orbiting Earth. Contact was made with the Gentle

Genius, the Super scientist Googol. Rescue efforts for a
Sparkling recovery are underway. Try to remember
we are Earthbound for now.

As I looked below at the landscape I did not regret being
Earthbound. It is still my choice, even though I prefer higher
places. We are taking over many Super responsibilities. We
are their substitutes in areas like the Malheur Wildlife Ref-
uge. Supers have defected in great numbers. Rainbows bolted
to LightHome by the millions or billions. Billions of empty
Earthens litter the ground, homes, collections and toys of
people. For now and since 1992 Earthens are inanimate and
inarticulate. Other Rainbow Dreamlanders chose their own
virtual reality. Many hollow Earthens about.

Pulstars are bolstering the ranks of the Supers and Rain-
bows. We outnumber them. They need us. The Earth needs
us. We are part of the Super-Rainbow alliance. Since the
Pulstars arrived, the Supers are retreating.

Pulstars are here until the poles tilt, an astroid collides,
the tectonic plates crash or any hot or cold calamity unbal-
ances Earth. Even then we might decide to stay for we can
weather some awesome storms. In2it pulsed Shebang and
Shergotty that the Cosmic Cousins are creating new orbs on
LightHome to accommodate Rainbows that might be dis-
placed in the future.

Supers have Avalon. People (and I believe all animals)
have heaven. It is quite reassuring to have an additional op-
tion on LightHome.

My stay radrodding at Malheur was a hopeful experi-
ence. I felt I could shed some light on this situation. I'm still
not too far from Bayhorse to visit a joynt and Jettison.

13

Virga, Violets and Violins

Jumping around connecting energy with lightening points seems plodding after awhile. I followed the patterns, listened to Pulse, tinkered with light-sculptures and rarely took down time. I was lonely and unrefilled. I was more than ready to see Jettison and jive in the joynt.

On my way, I checked the Pulse for joynt locations and offerings. Some were recreational joynts for sports. Some joynts held olios and tableaux, plays and poetry readings, gathered for critiques, classes and discussions. The joynt in Bayhorse was a multi-leveled, multi-purpose mine called The Underminers. Supers and Rainbows found many places to be. JOYnts are places to share adventures, make a friend, recreate and enjoy entertainment.

This joynt is still run by the LightHome returnees, all plastic without fabric accoutrements, former Radrods who light-paint to taste. Adit, Winze, Oreiard, Dixie, Stopes and Driftless greet guests, maintain the site and information board at the entry.

The list included categories for training, recreation, meditation, shaft surfing, discussion groups, library/archives access, performances, art galleries, courses in geology, cosmology, Earthenology, Superology, Rainbowology, any-ology you wanted.

Supers entered the joynt like virga, densified and flew to their special nooks. Supers come in many varieties. The fairy variety flashed past me. In one nook were dwarves discussing gems. Supers danced to fiddles and violins in vestibules festooned by glamour into elegant ballrooms.

The Wings performers were not due for awhile, so I listened in to a writers group talk about ways to energize their work. They talked about the VANGUARD system.

Visualize possibilities. Look and listen.
Attention. Absorb and avoid apathy.
Notice nuances and take notes.
Guard against limiting muse by early criticism.
Understand craft and surroundings.
Adapt. Pad and prune awareness.
Read and research.
Develop description with specific details.

Maybe I can think of this for my Waves, my notations. We need to write things worth reading. We need to do things worth writing about. Pulstars should have plenty to do and write about.

In an alcove a group of singers called The Shrinking Violets, one dressed as a petunia, sang a song about a lonely little petunia in an onion patch. Might appeal to lonely Pulstars, but they don't sit around and cry.

Art shows display light-paintings and light-sculptures downloaded at the spot. Artists swap ideas and experiment with forms and lighting. I admired the light-sculptures. They were much more advanced than my beginning attempts.

Wings had a pageant called "Pulsating Rainbows" scheduled for the next day. Finally I received a Pulse from Jettison. I was to meet him in a poetry reading alcove. He was reading a few of his own poems independent of the pageant.

I stood in the back of the alcove. Jettison stood in front with the poets. A simple light-painted rainbow arch hung above the readers. The audience jockeyed for views. But since the audience was only about twenty, seeing and hearing the poets was not a problem.

A solemn poet, who assumed we all knew who he was, read a quote which I considered arrogant and pompous, "A poet expresses the lyrics for the music of the spheres with pure, true sound. Rainbow words connect earth and sky enlightening the world."

Balderdash. I was not sure I was going to like this reading. I was glad when Anonymous yielded the stage to Jettison. Jettison, all dapper in dark purple, read his first poem.

What Do We Have?

We don't have flesh.
We don't have breath.
Our thoughts are fresh.
We don't have death.

We do have form.
We do have light.
Our usual norm
is to shine bright.

We don't need air.
We don't need water.
Our goal's to share
energy and order.

We do need guides.
We do need friends.
When our support slides
we twist new bends.

Then turning into a red-ivory pawn he slams the next poem. He popped up and down pounding his pedestal on a stone.

So What Am I Doing Here?

Burst upon the scene
as a sparky quark.
Filled out my form
ready to make my mark.

Learned the smooth moves.
Pitched a good line.
Dotted with light points,
cruising just fine.

When oops!
My bubble burst!
Illusions dashed.
Pinata popped me free and clear.
    So what am I doing here?

I could twinkle brightly on a star
or gaze at some cratered moon
or project my light in some undemanding dream
    dimension
or ride astroids astrally alone
or remain unformed in a black hole
Planet restoration is just hard work.
    So what am I doing here?

I want out of orbit
of this messy place.
Can't see the stars in light-polluted night.
Can't live in the open and be seen.
I am invisible. Unheard sound is my presence.
Oily rainbows puddle slick streets.
    So what am I doing here?

I wander observing this colorful, chaotic world,
send my by-lines bye-bye through the air
not knowing where they hello and land.
I wonder just who they might engage in conversation.
    So what am I doing here?

A poet who cannot touch.
A poet who cannot feel.
A poet who cannot connect.
    So what am I doing here?

I came to make a difference.
What change can words create?
How can I make this world better?
What impact and input works best?

I can question as I live here.
I can commit to experiencing life here.
I can muse on my experiments here.
From all the universal locations
and all cosmic challenges
I am bemused by the mysteries of here.
I hope I can make my life-spark sing,
bring a note of harmony.
              That's what I am doing here.

After Jettison's performance we listened to several poets and then left the alcove.

"I think you are improving with your internships. Where do you go next, Jettison?" I thought he needed much more improvement, but did not say so.

"My next internship is with Larkin in Solara. Then I have another internship with Musard also in Solara." Jettison had reduced the red to pink and was working on peach.

"I still have rotations in suburbia and mainurbia with a tinge of rural left." I envied his flights with Wings.

"Well, I envy you. I will be underground for quite a while. How can I be a poet when I can't at least surface from time to time. Maybe I'll only be a versifier." He envies me! How strange!

"I like v-words. Doesn't sound so bad to me."

"Well a poet uses more than v-words. I chose the name Jettison to jettison negativity from the planet. I've seen quite a lot of some people-polluted, climate-challenged areas that need more than v-words to describe them." He kept his middle name Pulstar to honor his origins, like I did.

"I've been trying in my notations." My v-titles for my waves could find me running out of v-s.

Jettison paused and we were at a standstill. "How are you spelling your name recently? Have you dropped the hyphen? More tidy, uptight, symmetrical, but with the hyphen it is more symbolic, more triumphant, more valiant." I like the glide and connections of hyphens.

"I've kept the hyphen, Jettison." I said. "Enough thinking like a poet. Time to think like a radrod. I need to tune into my instructions soon, Jettison."

"Oh, I hope you'll stay for the pageant. I have a rather important role. Not many Pulstar poets yet. Maraki Shiri let me help write the pageant. I need to go to rehearsal. Want to come along?" I knew I should stay. I had the down time.

"Sure Jettison, I'll walk you to the theater." I was not in the mood for meditation or being alone.

"Perhaps I can radrod with you sometime, Way-V. I've never been a Radrod. It might help jumpstart my poetry."

Jettison and I had some time after rehearsal to talk about our adventures. I did see the pageant. Lois and Osmunda are great dancers. Jettison even did some singing in duets with Maraki Shiri. I enjoyed the show. They have a small traveling cast since so many Rainbows are radrodding or rippling their own thing. They are clever in incorporating the audience into the pageant and the dance afterwards.

Wings was booked for another joynt and had to take off soon after the pageant. After a short dance, Jettison and I said our farewells and promised to Pulse each other.

The weather forecast indicates a bumpy ride ahead. The bigger the bounce the better. This was a pleasant interlude, but I'm ready to ride on.

14

Valuable Vanes

After leaving Bayhorse, I headed for the Columbia River Gorge in Oregon. She Who Watches still etched in stone, still watches. Over vales and under vapor trails, I am a vibrant viator.

I followed the old winding Columbia River Highway designed in 1917. This beautiful road with its marveous stonework and vistas was only used in its entirety for 18 years. When trucks took the road, traffic came to a standstill. Now they are trying to restore this rural companion to the river-following freeway to Portland, 84. Pulstars can follow either route to their destinations. I picked the right route for me.

Such gorgeous vistas of the Gorge! I saw five waterfalls at close range: Horsetail, Oneonta, Multnomah, Wahkenna and Bridal Veil. I stopped at viewpoints at Rowena Creek, Lookout and Crown Point Vista House.

I followed up Larch Mountain road above the cars below me to see my beloved mountains: Mt. St. Helens, Rainier, Adams, Hood and Jefferson. I tried to focus Check like a telescope to see the mountains more clearly. I focused the best I could. Cascades of praise for the Cascades. Wonderful! Near the outhouses, critters littered the trash barrels...not so wonderful.

I stopped to pop some points in a light necklace along the Columbia River, still a river of discovery. I needed to head south soon to angle into Silverton.

Farmers plant three-winged, propeller-like, silver, metal windmills to generate power for the Blue Sky energy project. There is a Green Mountain energy program also for sustainable power. Farmers can make extra money planting windmills. The power companies use profits for salmon-habitat restoration. In Albany near to where I'm heading the Periwinkle Creek Restoration replaced a culvert and restored a stream to provide access for young spring chinook. Renewable power and checks on emissions from the other plants, all hopeful signs.

I am fascinated by all the windmills and weathervanes. They don't whirl if the wind isn't around. I stopped at a weathervane at a farm near Mount Angel on my way to Silverton and the Oregon Gardens.

I stood at the tippy-top and rode it like the carousel they reportedly have in Salem. I had to shrinkwrap and magnetize tight. I slipped down so I could project and shape a light-sculptured finial of rainbow-swirled light pointing toward the stars at the top of the weathervane. A light-plume for the weathercock.

Since this Wave is so short, I'll call it a wavelet.

III.

Yellow: Sun
Suburban Scouts

Tamed Turf: Larkin

In bland, scrubbed neighborhoods
blocked boxes line asphalt sprawl.
Driveways lap across paved sidewalks
to curbed street.

In landscaped, trimmed yards
of clipped plants
pruned trees and shrubs
uni-height lawns—
poisons kill the wild.
Shears stab the untamed.
Weeds lurk to stick out their tongues
at the chosen, cherished
protected plants and protectors.

Nature conquerors design their will
to dominate their domains.
Beneath the surface
roots wriggle free
Above, branchings stretch boundaries
burst from bondage.

Fliers land to release growth.

15

Vital Vivifiers and
Vibrant Volunteers

The views of the Cascades lead me over the quirky and quaint town of Silverton with its shops and architecture appreciated by people. The Pulse informed me about my next destination, the Oregon Garden. Art nestles in seventeen specialty gardens and water features. Thousands of plants and trees. Some dwarf and miniature conifers. I prefer giant old growth. There is a 400-year-old Signature Oak. It is an Oregon heritage tree. There is a Native Oak Grove. Woods and wetlands for wildlife and plants. Rediscovery Forest, a working tree farm. Sounds great!

I flew over the Gallon House bridge, the oldest covered bridge in Oregon. The Oregon Garden came into sight. I headed to an old oak grove to receive my orientation to suburbia by Supers of the fairy variety: Trella and Goolkin. They were bonded. Their twins Larella and Kingol remained with their grandparents in Solara: Larkin and Googol. All the Supers need to reproduce to replace the defections from the planet.

Rainbows must recycle bodies and cannot produce more. We did have a limited Zoion experiment, but the warranty is up and only four Spectrals remain—Maraki Shiri, Kaiam Kaga, Beadra and Kisam. Their progenitors Ki and Samara are in Solara, Beam and Kaidra are at the Rainbow Redoubt. The Spectrals have not chosen to sparkle into more solid forms. They are like Super similitudes.

As we enter the suburbs, we face encountering more people in greater density. We also enter the favorite domain of the remaining Supers. Devas and fairies are devoted gardeners.

To avoid turf conflicts, Trella and Goolkin, along with other Super teams, will orient Pulstars. Supers will give out assignments through the Quads for available radrodding areas. There are vastly more suburbs than Supers at the moment, so there are ample Pulstar opportunities.

Slips, the Super protective gear, help them garden more easily. They have claimed the best gardening spots—organic and speciality gardens.

At the camp-in approximately thirty Pulstars showed up. Oregon is pretty well covered. Daisy Clem and Amani worked with Supers for many years. They laid the groundwork for Supers working with Rainbows.

The old oaks sheltered us as we inflated our Wrapps (some Rainbows capitalize the word Wrapps and others don't). I decided to begin to capitalize on every moment.

Pulstars waited for Trella and Goolkin to call us into our orientation. I knew Jettison was in Solara. Albedo was in a magnificent gardening community, Findhorn. Onterra pulsed from Alberta, Canada.

I guess I am destined for long-distance friendships. Maybe in my suburban rounds I'll meet new friends. But so far I'm a solo act.

Trella and Goolkin winged in their Slips into the group. They are slender fairies, matured from some of the images I saw of them in the archives. Both move gracefully. Both wore loose tunics of green-blue tie-dye. Both had blue hair at the moment as well. Supers are capable of shape-shifting their appearance and density from fairly thick to invisible. Trella and Goolkin were semi-solid, not see-through.

Trella began. "Welcome, Pulstars. I am Trella your Super guide to suburbia. My partner Goolkin."

"Welcome again. This is disputed territory. Some of it has been radrodded already. Some of you will need to leave Oregon to seek opportunities elsewhere. Some of this land has been nurtured by Supers for eons. Many remain because it is especially beautiful. Seek placements from your assigned Quad."

"But on the bright side, Supers are producing more off-spring again," said Trella. "Let us introduce you to our twins, Larella and Kingol— already nicknamed Lara and King. They attend Super school in Solara "

The proud parents pulsed images of Larella and Kingol. Fairies can age (or not) by changes in appearances. The twins were probably in the early grades of schooling. Maybe they were having first lives too.

Goolkin continued. "We tried to come up with a few guidelines for operating in Suburbia. Supers prefer to call this area Superbia. We are trying to keep it simple. Urban areas are more complex to deal with. You do not have the capacity yet to penetrate pavement—concrete or asphalt. You will need to dodge these areas in your pattern planning. Check mappings of your assignment areas."

"Here are some beginning suggestions," Trella pulsed the rules.

Ground Rules for Suburban Scouts

1. Wear your overcoats—Slips or Wrapps. Keep under Wrapps.
2. Check assignments carefully so you don't encroach on Super territory.
3. Watch out for lawn mowers.
4. Supers will be given preference for organic gardens. Pulstars can hang out in malls and lawns making their points.
5. Don't pet or pester pets or tussle with insects.
6. Approach Supers politely and respectfully, as you are visitors to their home.
7. There is usually less traffic on sidewalks than streets. Hover over congested areas and don't get in the thick of things.

Trella and Goolkin stretch and flutter their wings when speaking. They tried to keep grounded, but occasionally they would levitate a bit while making a point.

Goolkin seemed somewhat agitated as he spoke. "You are coming into closer contact with people. They are somewhat more relaxed in the suburbs than in the cities, but many have long commutes to their homes. They spend a lot of time in cars going to their activities and carpooling. The suburbs tend to be a bit more tidy in their yards and have fewer floors in their buildings. People are busy-bee beings honeycombing their hives.

Most don't believe in fairies, so don't concern themselves with our presence. They put growth enhancements and pesticides in their lawns and gardens. The worms, bugs and slugs don't have swift getaways. Lucky we have Slips and Wrapps. Of course our invisibility helps."

Trella's tunic rippled in the breeze. "The Super-Rainbow alliance is tenuous. Many Supers want to operate independently again. Now our numbers are increasing. We can reassume some of our earthly duties. We need to work cooperatively with the Pulstars as we did with the Rainbows before you to see that our relations remain harmonious."

Goolkin's hair darkened to cobalt. "Supers are rebuilding their bases in their mounds and in the suburbs. Some are still at organic farms. Ask permission for access in any Super areas. The Pulse will have maps of Super areas. Welcome again Suburban Scouts. Scout well."

They perched on a low branch then inflated their Slips for takeoff. Some grumbling in the Scout camp.

"Fairies seem to like manicured gardens and butchcut lawns. Less work for them I suppose."

"They lean toward conforming lawns and uniform heights."

"Most homes must be mini-hills for them to leapfrog over."

"Sounds too clipped, mulched, and composted to me. I'm going to see if I can be advanced to a city."

I stayed inside Check shielded by the comments. Soon the Pulstars consulted their Quads for assignemt. They took off in all directions.

I made no friends in this blip of a trip. Alone I consulted my Oregon oracle at Quad Four. I was going to a burb of Salem, not very far away from these lovely gardens I was not invited to see or tend.

16

Volant Views and Veloce Vendors

A golden statue called Pioneer stands on top of the Capitol in Salem. I wonder if the statue ever contained life. I wonder if it sparkled or went to LightHome. If people knew we had life maybe Pioneer would be the State Earthen like they have Western Meadowlark as state bird and Oregon grape as state flower. They sure did it right when they selected Douglas Fir as state tree. Maybe Portlandia, the Portland statue, would want to be State Earthen. If they had to select a State Super...oh this is getting much too complicated. We are a global outfit and don't need local recognition. I am a pioneer too on my own voyage of discovery.

I flew too high to see the marble monuments at ground level. A new development in south Salem with beginning lawns and seeded gardens needed some lightening points to get growing. A little energy boost.

The houses were all about the same size, mostly one story, with wooden or wire fences. I was going to be doing a little leapfroging or pogoing. It turns out many backyards contained dogs and cats. They thought I was an amusement toy their owners wanted them to fetch.

The birds on the power lines chirped and cackled as I levitated out of reach. I scouted out yards before impact and tried to place my points in areas without a patio, pool or walking stones. I knew I was not supposed to pet or pester animals, but I was not told they would try to pet or pester me!

Fairies sometimes haul slugs to safety if they can without people seeing them. I have no arms to hold them. I just have to watch them shrivel under salt and drown in beer. I feel so helpless. Slugs do not move fast enough to elude people. I try to Pulse warnings to keep out of sight and beer.

These proto-lawns sometimes come in rolls. They unroll the grass into place. Oregon grows a lot of grass seed and they have the rain to grow it. They have a need to conform the height of each blade.

I am not much of a gardener. My lightening points are my contribution, my seeds of light and energy. But I am a quick, nimble flyer. I fly fast. My element is to fly with birds.

In the suburbs there are many birdbaths and birdfeeders. I met a few birds (as they speak telepathic Global) and took a few tours over Salem on my down time. I saw the Willamette River again with the merry-go-round near its shore. I saw Gilbert House that once had a big collection of toys. I saw Enchanted Forest where earlier Rainbows gathered to ride the rides and see the displays of nursery rhymes and other fantasy figures and places. Of course, birds and Pulstars like parks.

I had quite enough of hide and seek with groundlings. My chief water source was the sprinkler. Sometimes I was chased under the sprinkler too. I learned fast that some animals can see us.

On the Pulse reported by Spig:

Pulstar chokes dog. While making rounds, a Pulstar was attacked. His Wrapp was punctured by teeth but quickly reformed for complete invisiblity. A man investigating the source of the distress could feel a lump but not see it. The man held open the mouth long enough that the Pulstar escaped. The dog no longer was blocked to the puzzlement of the owner. This whole idea of owning another life force seems so anti-democratic and anti-free will.

The pets are not entirely tame and conformity is not complete in the suburbs. Weeds of originality and diversity thrive.Despite my troubles, on the Pulse I heard success stories. Some Pulstars encountered non-pastel or white colored houses and well-designed gardens. Some steered deer away from tulips and roses. Some warned feral cats of dangerous areas.

On the Pulse reported by Span are some fun adventures.
1. Climb basketball nets.
2. Slide down drain pipes.
3. Relax and view the sky from a rooftop.
4. Do some bird and flower watching.
5. Peer in windows and watch tv. Help you understand
    what people watch as you people watch.
6. If you have limbs, tug a bug out of harm.
7. Walk in beauty. Don't just fly by.

I was ready to walk or fly to my new suburb on the plan. I will be more alert. My pattern wobbles because of intrusions, but I create detours. My next assignment is Philomath, a peaceful name, but then Salem is a peaceful name also.

17

Vivific Ventures in Variegated Views

En route to Philomath I fly over Marysville. Marysville is the home of the Larrabees (now just Laura and Wesley) who live in Rainbow House. Before 1995 Rainbow House was a happening place. Now it just houses Laura's inanimate collections. Rainbow House was the Rainbow Headquarters until 1995 before the Rainbows' exit to LightHome. Inside Rainbow House is Harmony House, the home of the original Rainbows, the Harmonys. Most Rainbows try to visit and leave a symbolic lightening point. I decided to do the same. I pulsed the Pulse for an accurate map of the area and zeroed in. Bullseye! I landed on the chimney. The chimney is not the suggested entrance.

There is a ground level entrance under the house. On the black plastic ground sheet many Rainbows light-painted their names and images. Many left greetings.

There were two Rainbow bodies. Both were wire and rubber construction with painted head features. One was just a sparkling possibility. One was animated and came over to greet me. She was the height of Onterra, but had black hair and brown skin. She wore a short red-felt dress with a wide white collar. The silent one was pinkish-skinned with brown hair, short-sleeved white shirt and short yellow pants with yellow suspenders. Both had black shoes.

"Welcome to Rainbow House," she said. "I am Marissa. I greet visitors when Burp/Rainbowlegged cannot leave his post watching over Laura."

"Hello, I'm Way-V. I'm a Pulstar. Who is the stiff?"

"That is the body for Burp to leave his red octopus body when he is ready to sparkle into becoming Octavior. But his tour of duty is not up yet with Laura. Come, I hear Laura snoring. She is very elderly now and naps long and often."

We walked into the green with gray trim ranch house. Burp met us in Laura's office. Burp is a small red-yarn octopus devoted to unrequited love for Laura. Most Rainbows have heard the legend of Burp, formerly Rainbowlegged.

Burp was an adolescent craft project gift of Laura's, then Hernstrom. Her collection of seven octopi languished on her dresser for years, eventually being shipped from Connecticut to Oregon after Laura married Wesley Larrabee.

All the octopi left their bodies on the computer (where Laura had them at the time) and headed for LightHome. The octopi, now actually eight with one more member, decided Burp should return to care for Laura when some Rainbows returned to Earth.

The Rainbow Chronicles tell of his struggle to leave the Rainbow Museum and find Laura. Burp did return and has remained with her since. She has no idea of his loyalty and unconditional love. He gathers dust on her dresser again amid the empty forms of former octopi. Only the inhabitants in Honeymoon, Laura's mother Honey's house, are Rainbows living in Rainbow House. Many collections, but they are no longer animated.

Marissa and I walked toward Laura's office (often called the Grand Canyon due to all the bookcases and file cabinets). "Let me give you a go-round. While we are in Laura's office, I should give you the Harmony House tour. Most Rainbows want to see some of the original Rainbows and founders of the Hub. Please no graffiti except on the inside plastic lining the doors." I wonder how long I had drifted in reverie. I followed her to the 50-plus room, five-level "doll" house.

It was a museum. Like a wax museum with the Rainbow founders layered in dust. The furniture was dulled by dust. The wallpaper retained a certain clarity. Some light-painting remained from before lift-off. The tributes on the inside doors shared the gratitude for the early Radiants and members of the Rainbow Hub.

Burp joined us at the end of the tour. Laura was snoring steadily now and he could leave. The spindly red octopus carried a dust cloud over his head which he tried to keep with him like a hat. He invited me to Pink Haven but explained, "Pink Haven is just pink insulation in the attic now. Not many bother to go up the Rainbow Chute. But at one time, this was the science center and gathering place for Rainbows."

Burp had a dust management problem living with Laura. Laura was not a duster, so Burp traveled with a dust cloud over his head much of the time for a quick replacement for when he returned to position.

"Let's show her heaven with Laura's over 2000 angel collection. When Laura and Wesley go to a play tonight, we can visit the Honeymooners," said Marissa.

"I'd love to see the angels, but then I mustn't stay long. I am overdue for my Philomath assignment." We hovered quickly to the room housing thousands of inanimate angels.

"You are close by. Perhaps you can drop in and see the Honeymooners then," offered Burp. "The Honeymooners sparkled me from my loaner body into my original octopus form. Marissa will help me become Octavior when the time comes."

I wasn't quite sure what to say. He wouldn't know when Laura would die. He was there for the long haul and it has been a long haul now—over sixty years at least.

"Marissa and I plan to do some radrodding after vacationing on the Columbia Icefield in Canada. She has been a good friend. She hides in the basket with me and we watch the Pulse together. Marissa helps with the visitors that still come quite regularly to Rainbow House. We enjoy visiting the Honeymooners. You'll like them when you meet them." Burp, when moving freely around the house, tends to move like a propeller.

"I'm sure I will," I said. "I'll Pulse you when I can come." Burp seems closed like a venetian blind in his commitment to Laura. Marissa told me he would not leave Laura for her or anyone.

Burp rolled along with us like a wheel without a rim. He talks no matter what pose he chooses. "Marissa keeps vigil with me watching Laura. I love the way Laura's wrinkles crinkle. She is pretty fit for an elderly woman. She goes to aerobics, eats lots of chocolate for energy and to keep fubsy, still loves lamb to vegetarian Wesley's dismay. She and Wesley still travel, see plays, enjoy grandchildren and great-grandchildren. Now Wesley and Laura are retired from teaching, of course. They are underfoot a lot. Just have to adjust my schedule to their sleeping and travel times. It is worth every minute to be with Laura, any time I can have with her."

Yes, definitely a closed venetian blind. I don't see how Marissa puts up with Burp. She's waiting for Octavior, I suppose, but that could be a long wait.

"Burp, you forgot to tell Way-V that Laura Hernstrom finally gave the computer disks for the Rainbow Chronicles to her friend Linda Varsell. Perhaps people will know about us soon." Marissa and I fly side by side to the table where we could see all the angels on the walls and shelves.

Burp whirled in after a few spins. "Doubt they believe it. Look at those people-sized rag dolls, pretend-people The Mennyms. Only the author of those stories believes they might be real. And she thinks she imagined them. They are fiction, not non-fiction like we are." Burp was flailing his legs in midair under his dust cloud spinning like a pinwheel. He could have been a helicopter.

"What will happen to these angels and Harmony House and all the collections after Burp is off-duty?" I spoke quietly to Melissa. The angels were dusty also.

Burp splatted legs akimbo on the table. Burp must have overheard for he answered, "Can't say for sure. She changes her mind a bit. Sometimes she talks of selling the collections or of giving them to descendants. The "dollhouses" could go to a museum. I know I will be free of Laura some day and it is not a freedom I foresee without profound sorrow."

Such strange guides to this house of Rainbow pilgrimage. It is almost a sacred spot to some Rainbows. There is a steady stream of Rainbows coming here and encountering these highly, unswervingly focused guides.

"It could be anytime, of course," Burp continued getting into a spiderly position. "Wesley is very fit and spry. Laura is slower and more retiring, but then she is in retirement."

Marissa shook her head. "Laura is really quite ancient. In her eighties or nineties, I suspect. Her grand-daughter Rowan helped her put up the overly abundant Christmas decorations this year. Laura does have someone come in occasionally to dust her collections, but that is another more annual event. Of course, her collections haven't been conscious for decades."

"I just love it when Laura dusts me. Sometimes she does it herself you know." Burp curls his yarn endings.

"I really don't know many people as eccentric as Laura who would care for such eclectic collections. Of course, I am delighted she was quirky enough to keep the collections intact all these years." Marissa nodded again at Burp all curled in comfort.

"Laura has taken such good care of us all. How can we not love her and want to be near her?" said Burp. This was getting a bit much for me. Burp is close to loony.

I toured some of the collection: Harmony House vintage 1950 built by Laura's parents Honey and Rollie Hernstrom. (Burp said that because Laura was so lovable, her parents built the house for her and provided the inhabitants who became Rainbows), the Scandinavian figures reflecting Laura's Swedish heritage, the corner cabinet holding her childhood dolls, various Earthling miniatures on the shelves, fairy and fantasy figures on the wood stove, elfish figures of Oregon, the gobs of angels, the Lucia figures, Honey's stuffed dolls on a rocking chair and more on a trunk, Rainbows with sunflower garb on a desk...the miniatures were toys (mostly in the Moon Room) and collections of people and animals like in the type tray in the bathroom. Porcelains above porcelain. All truly inanimate. All truly deadheads as Karen called the first inhabitants of Harmony House. Karen and I are of the pioneering tradition. We both are discoverers for the same cause.

"I hear Laura stirring. Must get back to position. Thanks for coming." Burp inflated his Wrapp and dashed to where Laura was waking.

Marissa and I rushed to the Rainbow entrance. I stood with her on the black tarp. I asked her, "What does Burp see in Laura?"

"Well, love is blind certainly in this case. I'm hoping some of that devotion transfers to me someday. Burp freely chose to remain vigilant to Laura. I hope he can sparkle into a new life as a Radrod when he is free of Laura. As to what he sees in her? Maybe a mother figure. Earthens are made by human hands and machines. Burp was made by Laura. He remained attached even after Rainbows could live more freely. His emotional bonds remain strong."

It began to rain. We were protected by the Moon Room roof as we hid in a flower pot waiting for the rain to pass. I asked Marissa, "Do you really think Burp can change?"

"He plans to sparkle into the Octavior form. Burp should at least change his name—not a very pleasant sound. We plan to radrod together. Whether it will happen and when is unknown. Love can't be contained, only expanded in his case. He says unconditional love can spread really big from even the tiniest Earthen." Marissa sounded sad.

"Way-V, Burp has been with Laura maybe seventy years. He'll always be devoted to her. He knows it is unrequited love and that it is me who loves him back. He thinks same species love might be even more satisfactory. But he won't leave Laura. He frets if she has a restless night sleeping or feels poorly. He fears she might put on her glasses in the morning and notice he is not there."

The rain let up as it usually does in Oregon. I felt I had made a friend in Marissa. I planned to visit again on down time from my assignment in Philomath. I made my obligatory splash of light on the green rock floor of the Moon Room. It was a rainbow swoosh with my name on it.

18

Venturesome Vassal:
Virdidity and Verandahs

Bouncing about the valley suburbs resembles a playground at times with parks, schoolyards, miniature-golf (not miniature enough for me), golf, tree houses, playing fields for people sports. There are sprawling malls encircled by lights and cars. The discount outlets, the big boxes of megastores, the fastfood boxes often with play areas for children are the squares in the suburban quilt.

There are McMansions, porches, patios and gated communities. The ranches and multi-level homes. Hopping place to place with no jolts to my form, no physical sensation, but internal thoughts volted. Darkness transforms energy to magnetizing light. I am like a battery ever ready for the next lightening point.

All the Rainbows are hop-until-you-drop busy. Down time is a quick touch to make your point then move on. Many seek more extended down time with others, away from the isolation and repetitive work.

I do pulse Onterra (currently in British Columbia), Albedo (still learning ecological techniques at Findhorn) and Jettison (musing with the Super poet Larkin in Solara). Sometimes I go on autopilot through a pattern on an enormous lawn and view the archives. Sometimes I listen to the Pulstation with Spig and Span or hear Musard and Glorian on Pulsations. I camp on stepping stones (if no one is around) and fence posts (if not occupied by birds). Winged ones, birds or Supers, tend to be territorial. I've been knocked off a branch by a bothersome bird.

I yearn for the company of a gathering place. Joynt. Joy plus nt equals Joyn't or Joy not? Or Joynt just another way to spell Joint? Joy and together?

Sometimes I do some tagging. I report the coordinates to Quad Four of some previously radrodded areas. I am not recording dates for the Earth has several calendars. Earthens began this life cycle in 1950 (on one calendar) when Karen began our liberation. Rainbows use various timing systems, but we are on our own.

Compared to the wild and rural areas, I find the suburbs too tame, too conformist, too neat, gardens too weeded, grass too uniform, gardens too pampered. Picked flowers in vases peer out from windows at the living ones.

While people tidy up and tame pets and homesteads, they lose control when weather causes floods, high winds and fires. Invasion by insects or unsavory others threaten. If they are too near forests, there are forest fires. If too near natural areas, the wildlife comes to nip tulips and gardens. The suburbs aim to maintain green. There is bark dust. There are also boundaries of fences and walls. But they can't keep out those who want to come in. I do like to dot hole to hole on golf courses. I do like some of the fence designs. Some houses go to strange contortions to avoid the boxy look.

I like sliding down drain pipes and scuttling along gutters. The colorful sidings often glisten with slug goo. Spiders interlace lovely webs. They break the smooth textures. People tend to flatten the suburbs. They let their pets prowl and I want to avoid paws or claws. I levitate when I see unleashed and uncaged pets.

Birds and ground animals munch on the flowers, veggies and nuts. This is a micro-managed area, but plans do go awry.

The fairies have staked a claim for the organic gardens. But they want more gardens to tend now that they are more numerous. I check before I land. We have to live with Supers, people and animals, but we must be careful how we interact. We maintain harmonics the best we can. They have to manage and steward themselves.

All our nanotech or nanos did not prevent one encounter with a very indignant fairy. Not sure what garden variety this creature is. From the vermilion grimace on his face, I could dispense with introductions and answers. Reminds me of images I have seen of the skinny Regal Eagle Rowan, RER. This guy sure had his wings flapping. Was he muttering in Volapük before sputtering into English?

"Check your coordinates. This is my yard. We get first preference for the organic gardens." Before I could check the Pulse, he was tossing a beetle and fussing.

"The houses around here are like gift boxes, presents we don't get to open. Everything's so square. We like rounds."

He was on a roll so I could not say a word. "We don't like weed killers, even when we are in our Slips. We enjoy weeding." Now he tossed some green tufts. How do you tell what is a weed? I wondered. Maybe it isn't a weed in someone's eyes.

"Some Rainbows have passed through, but they do not stay to assist, sustain and nurture the plants like we do. We are understaffed at present, but gaining ground. I'll report you if you don't leave."

When he paused, I checked the Pulse and spoke. "I'm sorry. I am next door." Not a friendly neighbor.

We did our work almost side by side as the lots were small here. I do not know if he still plucks and prods the plants there.

As for me, I moved on rapidly. Over a flea market with many inanimate Earthens flat on their backs like in a morgue. When I was near my next development, my flight was interrupted by a Pulse from Onterra. "Can you meet me at the Oregon Garden. Territorial disputes must be resolved with Supers. Trella and Googol are meeting Hugh and me. We could use your radrod experience and support. Meet at the conifer garden or if it rains we'll meet in the Usonian Frank Lloyd Wright house in the kitchen near the ceiling."

"I'll be there, Onterra. I'm due some down time."

19

Vindicating Vizards and View-Finders

As I flew inside Check, I pulsed the Pulse to find out what was going on with the Super part of the Super-Rainbow alliance. Rainbows returned from LightHome and Pulstars chose to come to Earth to help fulfill the harmonic role of Supers.

When Supers were able to SWEEP to their own planet Superior or ride out the hard times in Avalon, Rainbows filled much of the middle of the sandwich between the lower layer Superstars and the upper layer Supernals. The light-quilt quilted with lightening points restored energy at the surface.

Now the earthbound Supers were vexed. They wanted prime areas back. Rainbows were interlopers. Supers' growing numbers put pressures on wild, rural and suburban areas. They were not interested in the cities. Window boxes weren't much of a dig. They wanted to reclaim some of their former territory and duties. More Supers questioned why they could not work separately.

Some of the Supers were vindictive vixens and viragos. They had a tendency toward being supercilious. Rainbows hurt the vanity of the Supers. We could not allow this disharmony to fester. Supers wanted to have more representation on the Super-Rainbow Council. There is some muttering about this among Pulstars as well. Both groups outnumber the Rainbows who were here when Pulstars arrived and the Supers exited.

Onterra pulsed me in to the specific limb on the conifer. Trella and Googol kept an eye on the twins Larella and Kingol. Their vacation to Crater Lake was interrupted by the land use problems in the Pacific Northwest. Since they were in the area, and Hugh and Onterra were in the area, our governing body the Octagon asked that the foursome meet.

Larella and Kingol were flitting about, volleying a stone in flight. Trella cautioned them to stick close to the limb. I was an observer, ready for any questions.

Hugh, Onterra, Trella and Goolkin were already in conference when I arrived.

"The light specks freckle the lawns and are irritating to Supers, birds and ground creatures. They are everywhere it seems. It is like the stars have fallen. Googol says he is trying to invent a dimmer switch, so after the connection is made, the lightening point will be knotted, but not so glaringly," said Trella.

I was proud of my big splats from my ample bottom. Onterra replied, "I'm glad that is being researched. The nanos Pulstars brought did not include a dimmer switch. Supers will be working mostly in less lighted area. Birds can seek Super areas. Most of the ground creatures are mobile. They'll just have to move for now."

Goolkin twittered his wings. Today both Supers were brunette with sky blue-gray traveling clothes. Larella and Kingol were in tight tunics, about mid-childhood and red-headed at the moment. All four Supers had lean builds, long limbs, elfish ears. They had backpacks for foysom pellets for times when they didn't want to eat on the fly. They were in their Slips.

Goolkin said, "The territory problem is very serious, especially here where Rainbows have been a presence with Supers for many decades. With Supers' increased population and preference for this area, we have some serious problems. We face overlap. We have our own ways to heal and to energize. Lightening points do not lighten our load. To many they are a nuisance."

Trella continued, "Turf conflicts are going to occur until we can do very detailed mapping. It is going to mean Rainbows need to give up some areas. Supers want wildlife refuges, land trusts, Native American reservations, special gardens like the Japanese and Chinese gardens in Portland. We need to negotiate."

Shrinkwrapped Hugh paced on the limb. "I am in charge of Surface Operations, but I enforce, not plan surface problems. The Super-Rainbow Council has advisors to the Quads and passes along areas to be quilted to the light-quilt makers. Supers are part of this process."

Trella twitched her wings. "But there are now more Supers and Pulstars that need to have input. Rainbows have had cosmic assistance, but little direct intervention or individual attention. Supers and Pulstars need more attention."

It sounds like some vendettas could be planned if something were not done soon. Would there be vengeance?

Goolkin managed to keep his wings rigid. "We face too many overlaps and encroachments in this area. Maybe we need some reassignments. We need to balance jurisdictions and find the best land use for the territory."

Sounds like I may be hunting for another Quad. Supers want to hold sway over the most desirable and pleasurable places.

Onterra had light-painted her green and white checked skirt and white top to scarlet with a sheen. "This needs to be brought to Solara. None of us can do anything here. Surely there is enough room for all of us."

"Larella and Kingol," called their mother, "come away from the oak grove and back to the conifers. We must also keep in mind, now we have Slips, dwarfs and other underground dwellers are surfacing. Avalon is accessible by two-ways again. Volunteers are returning. With the higher birth-rate, we really need to have more space."

Hugh stood still. "We need to expand the Octagon to a Polygon and the Super-Rainbow Council into a new, true reflection of the changes not just here but world-wide. Planners did not anticipate more Supers or as many Pulstars accurately."

Trella and Goolkin nodded agreement. Onterra suggested, "Maybe we can Pulse Solara so they can begin discussing changes. When your family returns from your vacation, you can join Hugh and me in the negotiations. We can head there right away."

"There is such brightness and beauty here despite the rain and storms. Turbulence and darkness do not last forever. The meeting of air and water binds thought and emotion. We should be able to light the Rainbow-Super Highway together," said Trella. Trella and Goolkin smiled at the motionless face-paint of Hugh and Onterra. The sunny color hair of Hugh and Onterra shone.

The parents called in the twins. Soon they were heading south toward Crater Lake, considered by all species as a really beautiful place. I hoped we kept the same harmonic goals. We leave different impressions, but they are impressive ones.

"I noticed we did not include people in our plans, Hugh," said Onterra after the Super family left.

"Onterra, people consider it unsophisticated and culturally incorrect to believe in anthropomorphism or Supernaturals. We do not exist to them. They don't consider us in their land use decisions. You two have a good talk. I'm going out on a limb and pulsing Daisy Clem and Amani. They have worked with Supers for many years. They may have additional ideas to send to Solara."

"And you might have some suggestions, also Way-V. You have radrodded this area. Any recommendations?" Onterra asked.

"Life in the suburbs can be vapid," I said to Onterra. I noticed Hugh called her by her whole name now and his tone was more collegial. "I prefer mountains and high places. The city seems to be the hub of people power. We can share the areas the Supers will share. We will have our hands full with the cities. Many Pulstars haven't done city rotations yet. They may prefer city life now that they have their Wrapps. I have not done an urban rotation. I haven't done my Solaran stay either."

"When you finish your suburban rotation, come visit with us in Solara. Hugh and I will have to be there to help with the surface planning. We can take in a few plays, performances and maybe even one of Jettison's poetry readings. He might be getting better."

"Let's hope so..." I started to say.

A lovely auburn-haired fairy in golden overalls and a pansy spotted shirt dropped in. "I'm too late it seems. Guess I'll have to Pulse Trella and Goolkin. I'm Tanya, supporter of the fairy gardeners. Flew in from the Beaverton area."

Onterra made the introductions and included Hugh when he returned from his conversation with Daisy Clem and Amani. After some discussion, the four of us camped out on the ground and tried to find some solutions.

Tanya varied densities and fiddled with her Slips. The Supers in the suburbs of Portland were leery of any Pulstar sprawl. Tanya had a detailed map to Pulse to us. It was obvious Rainbows were not wanted. Tigard was also off limits to Pulstars.

"We need expansion room for Super operations. If Supers keep arriving at this rate, we could be near our former strength. We definitely need a division of land," said Tanya. Her mobility fascinated me. Her limbs and wings were so flexible.

"Don't forget water. We should be dealing with water rights at some point," Hugh reminded.

"Always a problem in the Pacific Northwest," sighed Tanya. "How I love the Columbia! Spend some of my vacations near and on rivers. Floating with boats, hang-gliding, water-skiing— paradise.

Tanya pulsed her points. Hugh and Onterra felt they needed to convene the Octagon as soon as possible to prepare for the Super-Rainbow Council meeting.

Fortunately I was heading south on my next assignment. I would have liked more time to talk with Onterra, but that would have to wait until Solara. Hugh and Onterra headed for Solara. Tanya flew back to Beaverton. I stood on the ground in the shelter of a root as a windbreak. I loosened my shrinkwrapp and inflated Check. Tally ho!

20

Vitalizing Vagabond

After my "super" experience with the folks at the Oregon Garden, I was ready to hit a joynt. Jettison pulsed that he was taking a break from Solara and was reading at a small (Pulstar mostly) joynt at Amity convened in a hollow log. The log was maybe ten feet long and maybe a foot in diameter. A rainbow light-painted the top of the entry. Inside light-painters left a warm glow of warm yellows, like candle light. I said I would meet him and he could tell me about Solara which was my next rotation after suburban scouting.

Poetry readings for all species rarely draw a large crowd. We had probably eight Pulstars radrodding the Willamette Valley. Five others came to the reading. No one but Jettison was a poet. Jettison was only able to read one poem before the discussion about it took over.

Jettison wore a light blue overlay over the torso on his pedestal with a cobalt blue hat sporting a rainbow band. We huddled in a semi-circle around him. It was a motley bunch: a silver plastic astronaut, a porcelain chess knight, a plastic infant in cloth diapers (poor pick for that life-spark), a plastic red bowlegged cowboy, a jointed plastic woman in a pink dress. And me. We all focused on Jettison, the guest. The visiting pawn poet.

How Does It Feel?

How do I feel about my choice?
My first life can be immortal?
How do I feel about my commitment
made in a cosmic portal?

How do I experience life
without certain senses?
How do I remain open,
in a world with fences?

How does it feel to be sick?
How does it feel to sweat?
How does it feel to touch snow?
How does it feel to be wet?

Yet for the loss
of physical sensations,
I do have some
mental compensations.

I do know how it feels to worry.
I do know how it feels to be sad.
I do know how it feels to love.
I do know how it feels to be glad.

How does it feel to be Pulstars
transported minutely in space
to enter a turbulent atmosphere
to have an immovable face?

I feel magnetic emotions
attaching me to Earth,
yet yearn for celestial connections
from my pinatan birth.

We never learned their names or where they came from.
The questions and comments began soon after the poem. It
was a tower of babble. Surround sound. I caught snatches.
    "I feel cheated not to have a more attractive form."
    "I feel lonely lots of the time."
    "I don't miss negative sensations such as illness."

"I miss being formless."

"I wish I chose Andromeda galaxy. Many more left the pinata for there than Earth."

"Frankly I'm bored being a Radrod. I better get some more rippling in."

"I'm leaving here for another rotation. I think I'll like the city better. I'm a people Pulstar."

Jettison and I just listened. The five left abruptly. Just Jettison and I headed more slowly to the entrance of the log.

I did not say a word. I thought, who does Jettison love? His feelings are rather vague. Maybe his internship with Musard will get him out of the airy-fairy feel he seems to have picked up from Larkin. But I did not want to discourage him. We are still newcomers after all and we need lots of practice.

I waited for him to speak. I thought poets can vitalize the language and life. I felt some spark ignite what I felt about being a dowdy, pale, limbless queen and restless Radrod. But I am also an artist, light-seeder, seeker.

Finally Jettison spoke. "Well, I really had a small, unresponsive audience. What did you think, Way-V?" Oh no, I need to think positive here.

"Good use of repetition and rhyme, Jettison." Maybe a stretch, but the rubber band truth would not break his spirit.

"Thank you. Larkin is rather dark a lot of the time. When I work with Musard and syllabic poems, I should lighten up."

We stood looking out our ringed viewpoint. We talked about Solara and all the theaters. But soon it was time for him to leave for Solara. I had one more yard in Albany before I would be heading south to join Jettison and the Super-Rainbow scene in Solara. I hope I do not have any run-ins with any Supers now.

21

Vivace Vindicator Vacating Valleys

Some suburban yards are mini-orchards with cherry, plum, apple, pear-apple, pear, peach, walnut, hazelnut (filbert) and fig trees. In addition to bushes and plants, trees present obstacles for Radrods to get around. I do enjoy ringing trees with necklaces of light.

As I radrodded a Pulstar-zoned, Super-approved yard with a cherry tree, I encountered six angry stellar jays. While making Waves, I noticed stellar jays on powerlines like notes on a musical staff. The six jays chimed one after another this chorus line litany of complaints.

Look there's a Pulstar glowing brightly
sprinkling light-spots on the way.
Keeps us awake daily and nightly.
Cats still chase the stellar jay.
We need a place to rest.
We need a place to nest.

Sprinkling light-spots on the way,
polka-dotting the landscaping—
we've not had our say!
Light pollution! No escaping
billions of points of light. Bah!
Saving energy for the planet—hah!

Keeps us awake daily and nightly.
Disturbs our travel plans.
Seeing dots in our eyes—unsightly.
Who do we see for bans?
World-weary, high-fliers plead,
don't send us what we don't need.

Cats still chase the stellar jay,
keep us from almost ripe berries.
We have to go out of our way
to peck at our favorite cherries.
Lightening points don't distract cats
or turn focus from birds to rats.

We want a place to rest
without those infernal lights.
Lightening points are a pest!
Get rid of these eternal blights!
We get our help Supernaturally.
Let us live light-free, naturally.

We want a place to nest
without light-litter all around.
We really think it's best
if another energy solution could be found.
Wings unite with one another!
Radrods, please **DO NOT BOTHER!**

The jays de-noted their lines. They left these lines behind them, aimed at me and all Pulstars. Sounds like catcalling.

"Eco-terrorist" "Light-saboteurs" "Light-weights"
"Cat collaborators" "Pestilent Pests" "People-poppets"

I ignored them and continued popping my points. For many reasons birds should consider less populated areas. I can't turn off the lights, but maybe we could dim them down a bit. They flew away before I could present a rebuttal.

My lightening points looked like buds about to sprout. I levitated the light to bloom on a stalk. I began to light-sculpt flowers. I animated the petals like pinwheels. My whirling light-flowers! I added color. Some were rainbow spectrum. Probably will really tick off the yard creatures.

I left my light-propelled, light-flowers circling on their stalks. My flowers dazzle in daylight, star-up the night. I will miss them in Solara—caved in an underground city with artificial light.

IV.

Green: Growth

Solaran Stay

Slips and Wrapps: Maraki Shiri

Flights come and go in Solara.
They return and take off so far a
Rainbow shooting star
beams light spectacular,
flies magically like a chimera.

22

V. I. P.

Reluctantly I left the lush Pacific Northwest for the arid Arizona underground. I had to visit the 600-year-old Douglas firs along the McKenzie River. The Rockies are spectacular, but the Cascades are my favorite mountains. Saguaros waved me into the entrance of Solara.

Inside the Solara protected area, I floated like a fairy by the glamoured and light-painted facades of this Super-Rainbow city. Lots of rounded structures. Parks with mushroom shaped tables and stools. Many theaters with readings, meetings, plays, volkslied sing-a-longs, performances of all kinds. Places to dispense foysom pellets—fairy fastfood for travel. Circular dwellings for the inhabitants who spend a lot of time here. It feels claustrophobic despite the high cavern walls.

I have researched Solara in the archives. Solara is the headquarters for the Super-Rainbow alliance. The governing and planning councils plus Science Center are here. Currently the surface planning is done by Rainbows Hugh (Radrod/Rippler) and Onterra (Pulstar). Osmunda is on leave dancing with little inclination to return to her Radrod duties.

Pulstars also working on surface planning are Lucid and Skylight (both have rubbery 2 1/4 inch Rainbow kids bodies). Lucid is orange-haired holding a painter's palette of all oranges. She has a white jumper with rainbow straps, orange tights and white shoes. Skylight is yellow-haired and rides a yellow paint brush. Skylight has white overalls and yellow shirt. He has yellow shoes. Both have white brimmed hats with a rainbow arch in front.

They are training in Solara with the aid of Mazeltov, a computerized robotic being. In2it brought instructions to create Mazeltov to Googol (the Super Gentle Genius) and provided upgrades for Beck, the Supernatural-constructed data processor. Two Rainbow Ripplers Angelyn and Nathane are working on the expansion into urban areas with Beck.

Overall planning is coordinated by Karen and Jorden and In2it trained Pulstars Shebang and Shergotty. Shebang is another Rainbow kid, but in green. He carries two buckets with green paint, wears green shoes and sports two yellow stars on his suspenders. Shergotty is a similar-sized variation in blue. White overalls, blue shoes and shirt, rainbow-swirled cap, yellow stars on suspenders and back. Intended gender-unclear.

The eight planners are called the Octagon. Eight angles. Eight sides to viewpoints. Karen, Jorden, Hugh, Onterra, Lucid, Skylight, Shebang and Shergotty: the Octagon. The Surface Quaternion and the Underground Quaternion conference in Solara.

There is a Super-Rainbow Council as well. The Supers will have their own separate governing body like the Octagon called the Super Council. When they work with Rainbows, the re-structured Super-Rainbow Council will handle disputes. Already the planners are working on territorial disputes. Trella and Goolkin are working with the Super Council to present the interests of the Superlights.

The Polygon will increase representation of Pulstars in the Rainbow part of the equation. I will be a V.I.P. (Very Important Pulstar). I am to serve a rotation on the Polygon from Quad 4. We are called Raps (Rainbow and Pulstar Service). I guess it is a voluntary vacancy position. No one gets voted in, just asked to serve. But how long? What are the duties?

When I heard my next rotation was Solara, I did not realize what I would be doing. I only learned of my appointment when I arrived and attended an orientation session in one of the large theaters called Ol' Sol. The Octagon was on stage. Approximately 200 Pulstars floated into viewing positions and pulsed in to the speakers. Pulstars dotted the air.

Jettison met me at the theater. To our surprise Albedo sidled up beside Jettison. To my further surprise Albedo was also called to serve with the Polygon from Findhorn.

Karen and Jorden welcomed us and invited us to enjoy the entertainment as well as the informational sessions.

Shebang and Shergotty reported we were working on urban planning. Most of the Rainbows were in wild, rural and suburban areas. We needed to make some innovations with our problems with concrete and other pavements. Googol and the Science Center were working on it. The Pulstars in this Solaran Stay were to study urban matters so all the Rainbows could be more effective.

Hugh and Onterra reported on the progress in the field. They were also providing information to the Super Council so turf-tiffs could be resolved.

Lucid and Skylight talked about their contact with Mazeltov (called Mazel) and about working with Angelyn, Nathane and Beck. They were processing a lot of data. Longer-term Rainbows and the newcomers: Pulstars all have free will, but they have to know their choices.

By Pulse, the four cosmic travelers decided to gather and chat. Onterra, Albedo, Jettison and I went to a performance joynt. The show was The Body Electric with the Super performers Leanon and Sparrow. What they could do with lighting and bold sound! They glamoured a new costume each song. They had a synthesizer with so many sounds, I had no idea how they found them, much less used them.

Afterwards the four of us met in an alcove to catch up. Only Onterra could sit. She curled on a rock which she light-painted scarlet. The three chess pieces surrounded her. I will summarize many hours of discussion.

Jettison was now working with the Rainbow Musard for his internship. He gave regular poetry readings over the Pulstation. He was not hitting the joynts, but stationed in Solara and broadcasting.

Onterra was the avid world traveler. She was getting along better with Hugh. He could be bossy if not gently persuaded to be more cooperative. Her descriptions of her travels made me eager to leave this cave and go global. She was not enjoying the negotiations with the Supers, but hopeful.

The malcontent was Albedo. Albedo the chess king in shining metal did not want much supervision. He gave us different notes on the harmonic scale. Some not so harmonic. "The affiliates of the Rainbow spectrum are splintering. We have the Supers, who have their own Super Council. We have the Radrods, both earlier Rainbows and Pulstars who are creating the light quilt. They need some attention to their needs. Monotony is a problem. Then we have the Ripplers, the other vocational and avocational aspects of Rainbow living. The balance between Radrod and Rippler time is a big problem."

Albedo told us the problems the Polygon faces. "The Pulstars greatly outnumber the 22,000 Rainbows who were here when we arrived. Pulstars want more say. The Polygon will try to provide this, but what is fair? We are all on the Rainbow Path despite our origins, but some see this mission differently."

Albedo spoke non-stop. "There is a group called the EER who are escapists. They are disgruntled Pulstars and frustrated Rainbows. They may escape into their own companies and work out their destinies differently."

Onterra, Jettison and I listened with concern. "Some Rainbows have Rainbow Hubs, small companies who listen to the harmonies and work to promote the Rainbow cause with little Rippler time. They are called EAR." EARS are a light note on the harmonic scale.

I felt a little better to know not all Rainbows were troubled, but then Albedo mentioned a separatist group, the Independents. "I am leaning toward the Independents, myself. We were not given the same wave-lengths with people. We have no mind-control or manipulation over people. They are responsible for the stewardship of each individual and the environment, just as we are. Indies just want to branch off on their own and live independently of people. I did my bit for people at Findhorn. I am ready for a company somewhere who will not be tied to people. I will do my time as a Raps, but I will not be researching the urban scene. Too many of THEM!"

Albedo would not listen to any of us. He said we each needed to make our own choices. "With our Pulse we can have open discussions on any matters that face us and can inform the Polygon of our wishes. We could vote on issues if we need to no matter where we were and what roles we were serving. How much leadership did we need as we swarmed over the Earth? We were oriented by In2it and ground planning was underway. Was the first liberator Karen still the Queen Bee since she started the Hub? Times change, does she still want to be? Should all Quads continue to plan together or separately? How do we share land with the Supers? I do not want to be here forever. When will they decide how long we have to serve, Way-V?"

We were all shrinkwrapped in Solara for an indefinite time. We had no idea what challenges awaited us.

23

Verbose Voiceovers into Virtual Reality and Vicarious Video Viewing

Living vicariously seems the fate of Raps. The four friends were on different paths in Solara. I had so much to study and learn. So many places in Solara to go. But we pulsed each other and planned times together.

Onterra and Hugh are in Super Council chambers trying to work out land use. The watery domain would be the Supers problem. We hoped they increased in numbers enough to cope with water. The Supers boycotted the cities, so by default Rainbows needed to find workable solutions there. The Supers are coming from mines, mounds, caves to slip into Slips. Once again they are gardening and dancing with the help from volunteers from Avalon.

Since Rainbows will be bogged down in cities with token presence in the less populated areas, many Rainbows were anxious. Onterra is a go-getter. She is good-natured and a peace-maker. But other Rainbows are less motivated.

Albedo is an irritant at Polygon meetings with his separatist ideas. He is forever delving into the archives for splinter groups and pulsing potential companies. He wants to have a new base of operations after his service to Solara.

Jettison is an earnest poet of mediocre talent. I find Jettison less irksome, but over-eager to please. He tries so hard to emulate better poets. He is my guide to Solara. He does his broadcasts and interns with Musard, but poets tend to be dreaming and musing much of the time. Still he makes time for me.

The Polygon meets daily, but only for about two hours. At present the Octagon meets with about a dozen Raps. Additional Raps are asked to serve on committees. I am the arts committee. I am exploring Rippler opportunities in the arts.

Jettison brought me to the alcoves housing Mazeltov and Beck. I wanted to know about creating virtual realities like the Dreamlanders have. Also in all their data collecting, what opportunities have they gathered?

Mazel and Beck were on their go-carts. They meander in the carts which hold their small, boxy appearance. The carts have four-leg and two-arm extensions. The limbs are so flexible. I was envious. The computer unit has two top buttons that look like eyes and the screen often displays bizarre facial features. They experiment in colors, number and shapes of noses and smiles. The eyes can be spiraled, dotted, puzzles, mini-canvases of strange designs in many colors.

With their upgrades, they can be creative. They can have and express feelings. They are not just data-crunchers, but two unique, robotic, sentient beings. They take down time to go hand in hand to plays and other performances. Lucid and Skylight, Angelyn and Nathane are not always with them. Mazel and Beck can work on data alone and consult with the Rainbows assigned to them. They look at it as a mutual partnership and consider themselves Rainbows of a different stripe.

Mazeltov is Babylonian for good constellation. Beck is short for beck and call. They love their go-carts and the mobility they bring. They love the gloved hands to connect good vibes and dance. Not all work and no play beings.

They are multi-purpose processors. They feed the archives, they gather data for planners, Radrods and Ripplers. They are synthesizers and analyzers. They are the incredible storage units for Rainbows' and Supers' knowledge.

In the upgrades, both have larger screens. Both are now three-inch cubes. They are the supreme communicators providing connections for the Quads as well as individuals. They are animatics, animatronics, animators of Rainbow lives.

So it was with great respect I approached these icons. Jettison knew them. He pulsed and browsed their incredbile web of information often. Lucid and Skylight were at a Polygon meeting. Angelyn and Nathane were doing some onsite city visits.

Mazel and Beck flashed their screens at each other. I could just make out some brown-striped, dandelion-looking, puffy flowers with golden tips on Mazel's screen.

When they saw us approach, their screens blanked flat, forest green. After introductions, I told them I needed to know how the Dreamlanders created their virtual reality. Has any information come in about artists creating virtual realities other Rainbows could enter and exit? How did the creative process work for Rainbows?

Mazel and Beck faced us with three purple noses and five orange smiles. It was a bit jarring. Their voices did not sound robotic or metallic. But then their go-carts might be metal or plastic under their golden, light-painted sheen. Their four silver legs and two arms might be some elastic material. The red gloves, maybe some synthetic?

Mazel answered my virtual reality question. Mazel pointed to the screen. Mazel spoke and printed on the screen erasing the facial features. "We know the formulas for the virtual reality Dreamlanders entered. Very few are left. They have a more active reality on terra firma rather than in their thoughts. Rainbow artists do not tend to create virtual realities to escape, but to create new art to share in the consensual realities we experience. They are capable of surreality and magical realism. We are not devoid of imagination."

Beck wiped the screen and addressed the Rainbows' creative process. Mazel's lettering glittered gold on green screen. Beck's displayed a brilliant magenta on green. "Rainbow artists dip into the cosmic consciousness. Pulstars bring galactic vibes. We tune into the planetary experience here and express our interpretations in the manner we enjoy most. Others might not see it our way, but your viewpoint is yours. No one can take your uniqueness and creativity away from you. Mazel, maybe we should take in the show at the Ol' Sol tonight. All this artsy talk just gets me hankering for some joy-jolts."

Mazel cleared the screen and covered the screen with an upside down rainbow of smiles. "Just a few references for Way-V and we'll vacate this joynt for higher voltage horizons."

For entertainment and artistic expressions, we were referred to the broadcasters: Spig and Span of Pulstation, Glorian and Musard of Pulsations in Solara. If I did not want to communicate over Mazel or Beck's screen, by Pulse or by archive, I would have to go visit the others. Cho for artists and Rascal for photographers at Quad 3. At Quad 4 there was Sequel for prose and Sylvianne for poetry. At Redoubt Kisam for light-paintings and Beadra for puzzles. I would have to contact Wings for their song and dance schedule. I was a Light sculptor. I would have to do a global search for other sculptors. I was given a web site for artist directories.

Mazel and Beck laughed after the listing. "You can check us out later," said Mazel.

Beck added, "We are on down time. All referrals now to the archives. Play time."

"We have a little while before the show. How about a prance in the park?" Mazel reached for Beck's glove. They were flexible, but not overly graceful as they bungled and bumbled out of the alcove in an awkward stroll.

"Now that is an odd couple, Jettison," I said.

"They are two-of-a-kind and the only two of their kind so far. Supernaturals with some Rainbow help created both from cosmically inspired designs. I hope I download some cosmic inspiration."

Jettison and I watched jouncing, jostling Mazel and Beck holding one each of their vibrant gloves. Neither Jettison nor I had free arms or legs. Jettison did not even have arms. Two carved chess pieces made for a game we'd never play. We have to play this game of life, limbless and out of touch.

Since I was Solara-bound at present I decided to visit the Communications center and the broadcasters. Jettison introduced me to Musard and his partner Glorian. Both returned from LightHome and entered form again. Musard has his old, white pajamas, blonde-haired rubbery form. Glorian was no longer the wooden angel she left on the shelf at Rainbow House's heaven. She was of similar constructuon without the pajamas garb.

Larkin, the Super poet was at a Super Council meeting. Sometimes she brought Larella and Kingol to the Communications Center to observe. Musard and Glorian shared Pulse time with her without a problem. She was interning more broadcasters from the burgeoning Super population.

Musard and Glorian said Kaiam Kaga still sent essays and stories. Sequel sent excerpts from his novel in progress. The poets Sylvianne and Svetla, other writers and artists sent their images and sounds. The Pulse was a visual and auditory communication channel with each Super and Rainbow an antennae to receive and send. We need never feel alone. We are only a Pulse away from someone.

Spig and Span said they were looking for more performers for Pulse access. Music, poetry, dance, art shows, plays, pageants, stories. Videos for travel and for down time of the various arts. Entertainment. Education with artistic flare. Expressions of all Rainbows and Supers.

I visited these areas several times gathering more information to share with the Polygon and to enter into the archives. When I was not doing Raps service, going places with Jettison, meeting with Onterra and Albedo, I would find a solitary small alcove and create new light sculptures.

Could I or should I add sound to my sculptures? Could I or should I ground or float my sculptures? Could I or should I leave them on the landscape or would they be light pollution? Should they be pure white light or how many colors should I add? What shapes could I use? On a flat surface could they bubble 3-d off walls or floors? City sculptures? Where to they fit best? What do I want to convey and say?

I pondered these questions as the days passed. Underground it is hard to know how much time passes and what time I am on— fairie time, people time, cosmic time? How much time did I have to work on the report? How long did

I have to be a Raps? I want to radrod. I want to sculpt. I want out of the underground. I want to surface.

Wings was due soon to produce a pageant in Solara. I would wait to visit them when they came. Maybe I could go with them.

24

Voluminous Varia of Vanguard

Just checking the Pulse for entertainment and connection is not totally satisfying. The underground is too confining. I am anxious for some above ground time, some peak experiences.

The Rainbows record their experiences in many ways and enter their work into the archives and the Pulse. We express images in different ways. My inquiry is to find out where and how they are expressing themselves.

As I drift around Solara for art opportunities, I twiddle and whittle images of light in front of me. Since they are transparent, I can see where I am going. My 360 degree vision does not seem impaired. I conjure projects I hope see the light above ground. Where will I place them? What will they look like in the darkness and in sunlight? How will artificial lights of the city effect their glow?

I am trying to get as much information as I can done in Solara. Then I hope to be able to go above ground to visit other Rainbow artists and writers. Maybe I will be released from my committee of one work for the Polygon, if my report requires me to leave. I want to find as many arts opportunities as I can for others and free myself.

Jettison hopes to inform his poetry, so he often helps me check the Pulse and visit dabblers in the arts. His apprenticeship with Musard brings me in contact with the Communications Center often.

Time just keeps going, but I am unclear the exact dating of its passage. I am on no time table. I am on indefinite assignment. Truly a go with the flow situation. I dream a lot about my radrodding time. I miss my mountains. My light sculptures transparently create in 3-D the images I loved and want to preserve. Mt. Hood. Three Sisters. Mt. Adams. Black Butte. Newberry Crater. The images flick in my thoughts and mind's eye in rapid succession. I want to be there.

But I am here in Solara. The artificial lighting of light-paint and glamour is just not the same as natural light. Jettison and I stroll the paths and roads lined with colorful curbs. Paintings decorate the walls. The outsides of homes can be like palettes with murals. There is an imitation of life as all art is. I want to capture the real and enhance it.

The Supers have their favorites which also draw Rainbow audiences. Larkin, the poet, goes in and out of dark phases. With the new infusion of Supernaturals, more poets should arrive.

Samara, the Supernatural musician/dancer with her Rainbow partner Ki, the composer/musician, perform as a duo and with their progeny Maraki Shiri in Wings. The Body Electric: Leanon and Sparrow draw large audiences. They even travel to joynts.

Live entertainment for radrodding Rainbows is found in the joynts. Yes, the Pulse provides vicarious exposure, but being in a crowd of wing-flapping clapping Supers and high-flying Rainbows is a real pulsating romp. The joynts have shows of paintings and photography. The artists and photographers often travel with their work. Sometimes I just want to escape Solara and feel the excitement of the crowd.

I guess I do get enthused when Jettison and I go to the theater for poetry readings, plays, musical performances by Supers and Rainbows here. The seatless theaters makes standing room for all. Since we can levitate, positioning for viewing is fun. My inability to sit is less conspicuous in Super-Rainbow theaters.

For our research we can project from the Pulse documentaries, dramas, concerts, comedy and art shows. We have access to the archives, people's internet and libraries.

Jettison tries out his poems with me before reading on Pulsations and the Pulstation. I have not been recording his poems in these Waves. He is so well-intentioned, but also kind of boring. Not that I am a barrel of laughs lately. I tend to get a tad restless at all the viewings and no action.

My action is going place to place to record the action there. Spiggot and Spandrel host Pulstations. Pulstars can share their first lives in poetry, prose, images. With our wonderful communication system there is the possibility of immediate response. The archives keep any inputs for later retrieval. Spig and Span are very popular with the Pulstars, especially the Radrods. More and more Pulstar Rippler moments are appearing on the Pulstation. When they do take down time, Pulstars volunteer to monitor the station for them. They do go live to performances elsewhere.

Musard and Glorian glean responses from the Rainbow Radrods and Ripplers. Musard with his pithy poems and Glorian with her more philosophical prose welcome the works of all writers. Many poems come with accompanying images and sounds. The arts are multi-media with the nanos to update the communication systems here. Musard and Glorian prefer to remain in Solara. Rainbows also staff Pulstations on a voluntary basis so Musard and Glorian can have Rippler time for their own writing.

I need to do a global search for Rainbow light sculptors. But I can't go anywhere yet. With Mazel and Beck, I am working on a website directory of arts opportunties. Jettison is helping with the poetry site. We both have our ideas for Visualizations. Maybe we can tour when we finish our jobs in Solara.

Mazel and Beck have incredible storage capacity. They assure me they are not even a teensie-weensie bit full. No fatal errors, hard drive failures, crashes of any sort. Their cosmic nanos technology is reliable. They have infinite confidence in themselves. They tell me that anything I find or store will be indelibly imprinted for others to use.

I like them very much. Rainbows are constructed of many materials. Most of us were constructed by human hands and machines. Mazel and Beck came with cosmic instructions and were built by Super-Rainbow crews under Googol's super-vision. Our life-sparks are all eternal and of cosmic origin. Mazel and Beck are a new way of being. I enjoy being with them.

While Jettison and I met with Mazel and Beck to research performance poetry sites I noted the performance of Mazel and Beck. None of us really sit. Voice commands get Mazel and Beck really nuancing the nanos. But most of all I enjoy watching the affection of these robotic creatures. The kindness and respect they display is truly a role model for us all. The hand-touches. The goofy graphics on their screens. The companionable words. The art of harmony. So many ways for the arts to express living. As the Polygon Arts Committee, I need to apply them to myself.

25

Votary in the Vestibule

When I am not the Arts Committee, tweaking light, visiting with Albedo, Onterra and Jettison, or attending performances, I am at meetings of the Polygon.

The Polygon meets to discuss the factions of the Rainbow Path. There is the Earth for Earthens Rainbows and the Earth for All Rainbows. The EER growl at harmony. EAR listen to harmony. I wanted to be a vedette for EAR.

I also want to turn in my report, finish my Raps career and fly out of Solara. I didn't come across the universe to perform indentured service. I came to free and to be free.

I am for diversity. Those who do not help or hinder the Rainbow cause, yet want to harmonically co-exist—to me is not a problem. If Albedo wants to brave the untamed wilderness, drop some sustaining lightening points, so be it. He prefers EER. I prefer EAR. But we can agree to disagree. It is not so easy at the Polygon.

Our cosmic orientation seems over. In2it focused interest elsewhere and left us on our own. In2it moved on. Pulstars and Rainbows must also.

The biggest challenges facing Rainbows is pavement and drop outs. We need to tackle the city and too many Radrods are becoming Ripplers too much of the time. I am anxious to radrod, but I am commited to being a Raps for now.

I don't do meetings. I do them, but don't do them well. I tend to doodle and drift into dreaming. Sometimes I tune in later for notes of meetings I actually attended.

Onterra held my attention when she and Hugh reported agreements with the Supers. The alliance should hold, but

115

governance will be cooperative and separate. Our meetings are all open to the Pulse. Lucky for me they are also archived.

Googol reports from the Science Center about working on air and water purifiers so Supers can operate without Slips, neutralizing oil and chemical waste, and especially for Rainbows—a zapper, a laser-like beam that can penetrate pavement to make more effective lightening points in cities. We can't bandaid the planet. However, a stronger zapper would be wonderful when we go urban. All these experiments are in the dream stages.

They have been successful in creating more robotic Rainbow processors like Mazel and Beck for service at the Quads. They are using the old Flock, mostly the Super Eagles and Ravens, to deliver supplies and Super-Rainbow scientists to construct them on the spot. They have not found a formula to enliven the Flock. The mechanical birds remain mechanical.

Somehow a formula attracts a life-spark to animate our amazing information, word and image processors. The go-carts give them so much more mobility. Their consciousness makes them more than nano-crunchers. We need more of them with their expanded capacity to handle the increased number of Supers and Rainbows.

Angelyn and Nathane report their adventures following the black ribbon roads and loopy highways. They balance on billboards and flit by the signs. They try to find ways to live in the city. They will be our orienteers when we are ready.

Googol has beamed Breathless with our requests. Both In2it and Breathless seem on call elsewhere. Googol wants our bodies to become magical wands, funnels for gathering light, zappers of pavement (asphalt or concrete), sidewalks and streets. Then we don't need to aim to leap from green spot to green spot, dirt to dirt. I doubt we can wait until Googol gets the invention workable.

Life in underground Super/Rainbow Solara is much safer and tamer than the above ground people/pet cities. Jettison,

Onterra. Albedo and I dream of different paths out of Solara. But while we are here, we enjoy being together and work hard on our enthusiasms. Can't bog down in the underground, for when we surface we want to soar.

26

Vivid Vignettes of Vintage Years

Time passes differently in the mound the Supers say. Since Solara is a Super-Rainbow city, it is hard to exactly place these events in time. What is important is that they happened to the benefit of us all. These vignettes I retrieved from the Pulse and also witnessed, deal with energy transfer and light regulation.

Rainbows are the conductors of energy from above and below the surface. We leave a light-stitch in the light quilt each time we make a landing in the pattern.

Pulstars came with the nanos, the technological upgrades that made our chances of success better. The Pulse made communication globally accessible. We could receive and transmit images and sound. We were our own information and entertainment center. We were the antennae.

We were the antennae to conduct energy to connect at the surface. Nanos made it possible to place the light-stitches farther apart and to mark them with a bright light. Our light-leaps bridged longer distances. Early Radrods made tighter stitches on closer patterns. When we do go urban, we will need these longer leaps to find green.

Our archives and robotic information processors are miraculous. Mazel and Beck are the prototypes for several more host life-sparks that are sentient. They can express their feelings and consciousness. We just call them Rainbows now. They have superior construction and capability to the people-made variety of Earthen Rainbow. We no longer consider them machines. They chose the middle name Nanos referring to their origins. Mazel Nanos Rainbow and Beck Nanos Rainbow now have eight Nanos companions—two at each Quad.

Two prickly problems that came with the nanos were too bright light tattoos at the lightening points which annoys birds, Supers and ground creatures. I was proud of my smooth, round bottom making such sparkling flashlights for the world.

In the scale of things the lightening points Radrods left seemed insignificant. They let Radrods know we tied the energy knot, left an impression. It was our brand and part of the quilt pattern visible to Rainbow and Super passersby. They didn't like our brand of the brand we burned.

But the light-dots or light-blots as the Supers called them were light pollution to them. Animals and insects found them too intense. We had to find a dimmer switch. We had to turn off the lights when we left.

The Dimmer Switch

Two of the researchers intensely interested in the dimmer switch were Googol's stupendous scientist offspring Strangelette and her Rainbow partner, a former Floater over Mexico, Damian. As part of the research, Damian sparkled into several different Rainbow forms to see what effect materials made on transference of energy.

Strangelette and Damian were the second Super/Rainbow bonding. Ki and Samara were the first. Unlike Ki and Samara, they would not have offspring. No new zoion experiments are planned. The Rainbow zoion experiment was a limited edition. Bonded pairs created thought-forms of a density unseen by humans (with their limited vision). These Spectrals and Changels could operate for the Rainbow cause undetected. But most were here only from 1992-1995.

All went to LightHome but four. Ki and Samara's progeny are Kisam and Maraki Shiri. Beam and Kaidra live at the Rainbow Redoubt with their progeny Beadra who is bonded to Kisam. Their other progeny is Kaiam Kaga who is bonded to Maraki Shiri of Wings. There are no offspring possibilities for these pairs, just like there is no chance for any Rainbows to reproduce themselves.

Damian and Strangelette (who Damian calls Lette) studied the different ways Rainbows and Supers transferred light and energy. Supers with their incredible range of shape-shifting ability can reduce to a life-spark, re-form at density of choice, transfer energy to others inside their Slips with safety and no light-leakage. Supers were super-efficient. No leftovers.

Damian in his multiple changes did not find any materials of composition made any difference. Damian made full-powered lightening points. Magnetism remained strong. The former formula did not seem returnable. Since it required more lightening points in an area and was less effective, it did not seem Radrods could go back to former ways. Radrods liked the longer leaps and the bigger patterns. They covered more ground more quickly.

The light-life of the earlier lightening points appeared to be seven years. The earlier Radrod marks faded. But the nano-enhanced Pulstar brand showed no signs of dimming. They needed to be turned off. A dimmer switch needed to be found so that after the connection clicked and the Radrod knows the lightening point was made, it will no longer shine. We need no fallen mini-stars on the ground.

How do Radrods dim the points they made and create dimmer points in the future? Supers and other creatures wanted the lightening points gone—pronto.

But the ways of science like in the mound move in their own time. The staff was small and limited to how much effort could go into each project. Googol focused on interplanetary communication. Cedar supervised construction of more Mazel and Beck prototypes. Zenon worked on a Bod-Prod to penetrate pavement. Fortunately Strangelette and Damian were concerned about the light pollution and light litter complaints.

Though many felt it was nit-picking, it caused a problem in Super-Rainbow relations. The less empowered lightening points had faded. But the bold statements of the nanos-enhanced variety were like light-punches.

Strangelette in her Slips and Damian in his Wrapps went on a field trip to an area polka-dotted by an overeager Radrod. It was as if the Radrod danced a crazy quilt all over a suburban backyard. The Super superintendent wanted to restore this organic oasis to its natural state.

"Some deranged Radrod sprinkled some monster-sized stardust all over MY yard beside MY garden!" the Deva was a diva in full voice. She flitted about stomping and flapping her wings. She was MAD! Her density thickened and thinned. She was crimson all over. She was in a twit.

"What are Radrods doing here anyway? Organic gardens are OUR domain. Flowers turn their petals away from the lawn. They will get a crick in their pedicel. Their flowerage is blighted. Oh think of the stigma!" She was really in a rage.

Damian was the fall guy for the Rainbows here. "Perhaps some map mistake? But the pattern does seem erratic and too closely stitched. I'm sorry for the inconvenience."

"Inconvenience! These are intolerable work conditions. I will need a new assignment. I cannot work here Slips or no Slips." The Deva blinked out and in with indecision. Finally the Deva abandoned the area.

Damian and Strangelette stayed and used the lightening points for experiments. Tweaking formulas and energy flow. They gardened with the lightening points until the lawn looked really odd. The points varied in intensity. Light-painting and glamour were not very effective. They caked the points with the make-overs, but the blemish remained. They tinkered until some of them dimmed. They diligently made modifications so they could dim Damian's landing light with a timer that would fade the light off. They pulsed the formula to every Rainbow so Radrods could make their points less brightly. Radrods could know the light would go off.

But what to do with the bright spots already made? They could be like the eternal flames people torch. They were able to mute Damian's spots, but the light-dandelions would not puff and blow away. Damian, currently in a jointed plastic form sat amid the lightening points with Strangelette wondering what else to do.

"Lette, our nanos did not anticipate this problem. Our Cosmic Cousins are not exactly on call. I don't know what else to try."

After a slight pause Strangelette decided to contact the Superstars. Lithania at the Council Chambers in Solara had access to the Superstars. They abandoned the light-blight and headed home.

Lithania with her penchant for florals in orange, orange culottes with orange petunias on her wing tips made the contact with Lucifer and Lilith in the interior. When they explained the problem, the Superstars did not consider it a problem.

"We have maps of the light quilt patterns since we send energy to the sites. They are dated. We can pinpoint the new lightening points and dowse the light. The connection is made. The light is just excess energy," said Lucifer, a very luminous Super in faint blue.

"We will get our technicians zapping right away. It is just a slight computer program problem," added the equally splendid Lilith.

When Strangelette and Damian reported the news to the Pulse, many Radrods went back to their former quilting grounds just to see if indeed the lights were out. They were happy the new formula turned out their lights for them. Supernatural technical skill saved the Rainbows again.

Ironically the ineffectiveness of the lightening point was also a problem. We were going urban and the pavement was a barrier to our success. All the scientists in Solara turned their attention to the problem. We were hopeful since we solved the dimmer switch that we could find the formula for the Bod-Prod.

No matter how many times Googol, Zenon, Cedar, Strangelette, Damian and the other scientists tried to dip into the cosmic consciousness, no matter how many times they pleaded to the Cosmic Cousins for assistance, no matter how many experiments they tried, they could not invent a way a Rainbow body could prod through pavement. We needed a Bod-Prod to penetrate the lightening point through pavement either from above or below to connect the energies at the surface. We were having a hard time working out our urban designs. Park to window box (which did not work well for off the ground), was not delivering enough of the energy grid. Breathless came to our rescue once more. In2it was off somewhere.

The Polygon met for a regular session. Our alliance with the Supers maintained harmony between us. We were tackling some minor land use complaints when a flickering bluish to purple light flashed in our midst. Breathless had arrived in our mostly arid underground.

The Bod-Prod

The light flicked with the sounds of the words. Our dedicated Cosmic Cousin sounded concerned. He addressed his special friend, his beloved Rainbow Jorden—one of the overall planners with Karen, Shebang and Shergotty.

"Ah, Jorden the weight of the world on such tiny beings. The universe will provide and assist. Harmony is achieved in many ways. Be prepared to intervene and assume responsibility for a larger task." The light blinked intensely.

"You need to go urban urgently. The Supers are equipped for unpaved areas. You need an energy delivery system for pavement. You will have to go around buildings for now, but you can penetrate sidewalks and streets. Be careful you do not end up a splat in the foot and wheel traffic." Breathless flickered toward deep purple.

"The Cosmic Council sent me to deliver the Bod-Prod. Your bodies can conduct a laser-like beam that can arrow in cosmic energy through the pavement to connect to the energy from the Earth's core. The lightening point will not add to the light pollution of the city. Radrods will know contact has been made when a dull gray stamp appears on the pavement. The stamp which is a simple R will fade within minutes. You will be swords of light." The light became spiky.

"Ah Jorden. I'm feeling soggy even as I flick off the dampness with these light-flashes. I'll squeeze myself out.

It is strange to get attached to this boggy-down place when so many arid opportunities await me. But I endure moisture for your sake, Jorden. I hope our galactic paths cross soon."

"Maybe we could build a fire to dry you out faster, Breathless. You have been a true friend to us. We are so grateful for all you have done for us." Jorden looked up toward the pulsating light as we all were with intense appreciation. Jorden shouted to the light with the best volume he could muster.

"Thank you, Breathless. Do come soon. Come see how the Bod-Prod works. Everyone on this planet appreciates your concern, even if they don't know about it."

"I evaporate well, Jorden. No need for a fire. It is a preference, not a necessity to remain dry." Breathless dimmed.

A pinprick, barely visible answered, "I will return, Jorden."

Googol pulsed the formula to all Rainbows. We could do a bang-up job in the cities. I do not know when I will get there, but when I get there I'll do so with a bang.

This increase in light capacity could help me with my light sculptures. I needed to leave behind light-art that enhances, not detracts from the environment.

With these nanos advances, Rainbows can help steward the Earth more effectively. We should have less Radrod burnout. Supers can make their energy transfers in their manner. Rainbows have better ways to energize their light-quilt.

These changes lead me to want to complete my arts survey as soon as possible. After talking with Maraki Shiri about her encounters, I will be ready to take my art globally perhaps to share my visualizations directly, on the spot.

27

Vengeful Vassal Voted Out

At the end of a session of the Polygon discussing our plans to begin serving urban areas, Albedo asked to address the Polygon. "I want to be released from Raps duty. I have made contact with Dawna in the Tumucumaque Mountains National Park in Brazil. She has developed an EER enclave there. Supers can have plenty of space in the 9.6 million acres of forest-covered mountains with granite outcroppings. They rise 2,300 feet over the forest canopy. There is a treasure trove of undiscovered plants, animals and insects protected so people can't destroy them. It is the world's largest tropical national park. It is one of the most pristine forests remaining. I'd like to keep these 350 birds species, 37 types of lizards, eight primate species and oodles of plants safe for biodiversity. I want to find new life forms."

I thought mountains, how lucky for him. I thought Brazil, so far way, but I can visit...someday.

Albedo showed some pictures of the animals over the Pulse. We really have not done much with animals. Supers have done most of the animal care and intend to keep it that way. I saw strange animals— different from the choices we saw coming across the universe for life options after the pinata pop. Black spider monkeys (really limber), harpy owls (really vigilant), anteaters and giant armadillos (really weird), jaquars (really sleek) and sloths (really not that appealing). They have 200,000 square miles to roam and I can't leave Solara.

Albedo showed us moving images of white water rapids, the waterfalls, impassible rivers for most people. The area is mostly untouched by people (hurray). That is just what

Albedo wants—no people, just as we are about to go into urban areas. This is virgin rainforest, virtually uninhabited by people in Amapa State. A paradise for Albedo. An escape route from the Polygon's perspective. The Polygon needs his help in the polluted, populated areas.

Albedo spoke again. "There will be new species to discover. No pesty people. Live and let live philosophy. There is no rust with shrinkwrapps. Whatever metal my nuts and bolts are made of should weather well. I did my people-propping time at Findhorn. This is the wilderness. We stake our claim to this domain for Rainbows to share with Supers. This is maybe the world's last roadless wilderness. Deforestation is destroying the Amazon. This area is under protection and sustainable development reserves. A safe haven where Rainbows of EER persuasion can live in peace. No lightening point polka-dotting the landscape."

Hugh stood and faced the Polygon congregation. "Of course you have free will to go, Albedo. You seem to feel vengeful toward people and you do not want to radrod lightening points. Since you do not want to participate in the Rainbow harmonic mission, I suggest we take a vote to see if Albedo should remain a member of the Polygon."

Shergotty spoke next. "I am embarrased for the hardworking Pulstars to see you shirking your duties. I am working on the overall plans. You did not consult us about the EER's plans."

Albedo said, "Because I am not asking to be included in your plans. I am not asking your permission to go. I am telling you my intentions. Take your vote. It is meaningless to me. Regardless of your vote I am leaving. The EER will live harmoniously with nature, with any Supers or Rainbows who choose to visit or stay. My people-poppet days are over."

I voted for him to leave, just so he could leave his position legally. It really did not matter to Albedo what the vote was. But it sets a precedent for free will and for commitment to the cause we came for. But then it is still a way of life not detrimental to the planet.

Albedo pulsed Jettison, Onterra and me to meet him in an alcove to say farewell. We faced inward in a circle. Albedo spoke first, "I'll take the highlands and you take the lowlands and we'll meet on our down times."

"I'll need to see when Hugh's and my travels go to South America. Not much of a chance Hugh will want to see you. But I think you have the right to your decision and I wish you well. The rainbow has more than one stripe in the spectrum," said Onterra. She is the only one with arms to hug Albedo.

"Jettison and I will be here forever it seems. But we dream of a global Visualizations tour. Can't think of a more exciting place to be. I won't litter it with light sculptures." I was so envious of the mountains. I wished I could leave with him.

"This energy infusion work we are doing to stabilize the impact of Earthlings on the planet, may not work. You are going to an area where you might observe sustainable solutions," said Jettison.

"Yes, if the people botch it up, the planet is ours until the Cosmic Cousins find another life force to complicate things a bit. I just want to live where people have left good deeds, not bad deeds. This might be a place for the Repulstars to wait for reassignment," said Albedo.

"Repulstars?" I had never heard of them.

"When I was looking for relocation sites, I learned of a group of Pulstars, who wanted to return to the cosmos for reassignment. They felt they made a mistake coming here. They wonder where is the Pulstar back-up? Is our blast a permanent placement? One choice and no out? They are repulsed by conditions here. They are waiting for instructions how to disembody their life-sparks to the universe for reassignment without becoming a directionless Floater. We know how to ground Floaters, but not get them off to another planet for reassignment." Albedo shone with excitement.

Albedo asked questions each of us answered differently for ourselves. "Why not live openly without need of camouflage, without interference by people? Why not consolidate an area for ourselves?"

"I'd feel I was desecrating the wilderness with my light sculptures. I need to find places where they would be welcomed," I said.

"I'm sure I'd be inspired to write poems there," said Jettison. "I'd like a larger audience."

Onterra placed her hand on Albedo's head bolt. "I wish you well. I am committed to surface planning. I am replacing Osmunda. I wish there were more areas like this I did not have to plan for."

"Tumucumaque means 'the rock on top of the mountain.' I intend to be such a rock for ages." Albedo began motions to leave.

We reminisced about our space travel, our meetings and times enjoying the entertainment of Solara. I'd miss our discussions even though the four of us have some dissonance.

We hovered closely to the green-light-lined route to near the entrance. I watched Albedo hover, dodge and dart in a rollar-coasting way out of the entrance of Solara.

He headed south, but I no longer followed his flight to Amazon adventures with the EER. He would miss our new show: El Arco Iris.

28

In Vogue Vaudevillians

El Arco Iris is a variety show, vaudeville. We look like ventriloquists with our immovable faces. Actually we considered it a Fantoccini, a stringless puppet show.

My contributions to the production were seven, rainbow-striped light pillars. The pillars were about three feet tall which is tall for us and the highest I had extended light.

Another artist in the Solaran stay was Nytanu. Nytanu was three and 3/4th inches—all plastic. Only his blue eyes and red lips retained color. His pants have only traces of blue. He was pink plastic with arms which hug his belly but are unable to hang free of his form. On his back it said Best USA.

Since Nytanu and I both had functionless arms, we understood the challenge of an artist without limbs. Nytanu wanted to focus and tweak photos for the Pulse. He also wanted to travel globally and record for the Pulse and archives the many beautiful places on this planet. He wanted to transmit in 3-D.

We talked a lot about technique and how I made my sculptures. Soon Nytanu and I were fast friends. I spent as much down time with Nytanu as I did with others.

After months of trying, we could not conjure his images over the Pulse in 3-D. I could not transmit my sculptures in 3-D either. The Science Center had many other projects considered more important. It could be a long time (or never) before our 3-D dreams would be realized.

Nytanu tried to make his photos bulge from flat surfaces. He had some success, but it could not go over the Pulse three-dimensionally. We both struggled with our projections.

The day came when Nytanu could wait no longer. I met him off stage at the theater where the cast was rehearsing.

"Way-V, I decided it is time to go. I can't wait any longer. I will store my photos and hope I can transmit them some-day over the Pulse as they should be seen." Nytanu paused. "Would you consider coming with me. We could experi-ment and maybe someday our art will reflect our explora-tions."

I thought, Wow a chance to go globally! A travel com-panion that understands what both of us are attempting. Our unmoving visages conceal deep emotion. I really liked Nytanu. He was such a good artist. Why not go?

After a pause I had to answer. "Nytanu, I am not free to go yet. I have an urban rotation and I see my work brighten-ing the cities. You will capture the special moments in a changing world.

I need to create special moments in my art. I am not ready yet. I am not fully trained."

"I understand. But it is time for me to leave. I will keep in touch, Way-V."

As he left, I felt very sad. We shared our art and our lives. Pulsing is just not the same. Friends have to let the other go, sometimes.

I went into the audience to watch the rehearsal. I tried to cheer up as the cast did their best to entertain. When I thought "best" I remember the words on Nytanu's back. Someday he would earn that name.

Jettison saw me in the audience. He could not tell my mood for I had no expression. But when I spoke to him about losing a friend, he tried to cheer me up.

Soon the rehearsals were over. Nytanu pulsed some pic-tures from the Alaskan glaciers. I stored the pictures for later viewing. Occasionally we talked over the Pulse. There were no technological breakthroughs to 3-D for us.

I put the final tints on the pillars and soon it was showtime. The production was to go world-wide on the Pulse. Besides the seven pillars the only staging was a blue backdrop. In golden neon light it said El Arco Iris, A Fantoccini.

The announcers are Musard and Glorian and Spig and Span. They banter and joke between the seven acts. Then audience and Wings cast create a pageant called El Arco Iris which incorporates all the performers. I recorded all the acts for viewing later. The seven acts are:

1. Leanon and Sparrow: The Body Electric. Surreal Super Gig.
2. Poetry Reading by Larkin.
3. Poetry Reading by Jettison.
4. Ki and Samara: satirizing a song and dance act.
5. Dance solo by Osmunda.
6. Dance solo by Lois.
7. A pageant co-created with Wings.

Jettison wanted me to record his reading, so he could see how he did. He was all into the theme with a rainbow hat band on his golden hat. His torso was gold. His pedestal was a rainbow-striped, ribbon-like snake spiraling around it. All the costumes were playful and over the top. It was for fun. I even sported some colorful dots on my dress and bands on my bonnet.

Jettison prepared two poems. He memorized them and delivered them with overblown diction. Levitating on several occasions for emphasis.

Thingness

Am I the thingamabob,
　　the daub right for the job
　　　　or some sentient fob?

Am I a thingamajig
　　that's right for this Earthen gig
　　　　or some cosmic thimblerig?

Maybe I'm a thingummy?
    (now that sounds flunkydom-y)
        perhaps a bit too humdrummy?

Maybe I'm a thing-in-itself
    destined for some mantel shelf?
        I prefer Pulstar myself.

I Make No Sense

People make sense (so they tell).
Unlike me, they can smell.
They can eliminate waste
and some have good taste.

They focus sight through their eyes.
Narrows their vision, I surmise.
They funnel sound through their ears.
An Earthen telepathically hears.

I have surround sound and sight.
I magnetize and project light.
We all have operations to think.
Our mask-like faces do not blink.

I feel through thought not sense.
Other splendid gifts recompense.
I gather experience from surroundings.
Make sense like Pulstar foundlings.

I guess being moist and fleshy
tends to make Earthlings more messy.
I guess being more solid
makes Earthens less liquid.

But the sense I value so much
would be the sense of touch.
To feel each diverse texture.
To know the temperature.

I create light and thought projections.
I make my close connections.
Love for Pulstars I find
is pulsed mind to mind.

We all experience life our own way.
Which way is best, I can't say.
We all make sense most of the time.
I hope's that's true of this rhyme.

The pageant involved the audience in singing and dance sequences lead by the Wings cast. Since it was a Super-Rainbow production, both groups made their special contribution. I discovered Jettison could sing and dance better than write poetry. Despite our rather inflexible forms, we could bounce about like the others.

When the show was over, I interviewed Maraki Shiri and Kaiam Kaga about their perception of the arts scene for Rainbows. Maraki Shiri and Kaiam Kaga are sheer and graceful compared to clunky chess pieces. They were gracious also. My report data mushroomed.

I also spoke to the dancers Osmunda and Lois. It was obvious Osmunda's leave was permanent. She had no intention to return to travel with Hugh. Lois was also a Rippler for dance. Neither wanted to radrod. Both gave dance instruction over the Pulse and in workshops in joynts.

Jettison and I went to a park and faced a mural. "Jettison, I think my report is complete enough to take some down time in the mountains. I want to do some light-sculpting and prepare for some city radrodding. Do you think I can leave my Raps assignment? I surely do not want to leave like

Albedo. I'd like to leave like Nytanu, thinking I can be ready for any challenges"

"I'm heading for an internship with Svetla next. But I'd like some down time. Can I come along to the mountains with you? I've been cooped up too long in Solara. I'd like some new experiences for my poems."

Jettison and I made a dash for the headquarters of Karen and Jorden. Since we do not sleep, we are fairly sure if people are where they are apt to be, we can find them. I pulsed ahead to see if they were available.

Karen and Jorden met us in front of headquarters. The rainbow arch over the door was the only decoration. When we made our requests, they were granted. We were on leave for some mountain time before reporting for our next rotations.

As Jettison and I inflated Trope and Check (after shrinkwrapping ourselves to talk with Jorden and Hugh), I saw Jorden take Karen's hand as they strolled into the open door. The companionable way they talk to each other and the ability to hold hands was wonderful to see. The two intouchable chess pieces made their moves toward the mountains.

V

Blue: Dreams

Majestic Mountains

Mountains: Sylvianne Rippler Rainbow

Wild
mountain
sentinel
peeks at rainbows.
Cold-clad, meadow specked
water-carved, jagged crags.
Wind, weather, bend and tussle.
Stitched with light-quilt to hold
Earth's knuckles; defiant fists upward.
Volcanoes mouth openings to universe.

Sky-
seeking
pinnacles
cloud-punching peaks
star-gazers' viewpoint
galactic probe-pointer
Gaia's thrusts from crusty core
cosmic poker of mystery
bumps of planetary destiny
reveal wholeness, connection and oneness.

29

Varnishing Veracity: Vegetable Ivory

Jettison and I beeline for the Cascades. Snow-covered slopes near chair-lifts at Hoodoo meant skiers, snowboarders and teleboarders meandered at various speeds up and down the mountain. We hovered above them. No snow blocking our view. Our Wrapps were varnished into a shield. Our shrinkwrapps have a more patinaed finish.

Some snow-bundled people prefer snow skates and snowshoes. We watched them stride, glide and plod across the snow. Still others made snow people, threw snowballs, basked in the sun outside the lodge.

Jettison and I came to the mountains to explore our truths and our arts. What kind of vision can we gain from such spectacular vistas?

My time in Solara made me feel I was vegetable ivory—not the real deal. I had little time for my own art while I was being a Raps and the arts committee. There were no volunteers to delegate my duties to so I could be a Rippler for awhile.

Jettison and I found a people-free zone to settle our Wrapps to camp. We were free of the cave. The horizon was clear. We could bubble on the surface and dream. People have day dreams and night dreams. We don't sleep so we can dream—whenever. Jettison rolled in the snow inside his Wrapps. He'd roll along a limb and plop in the snow. Shrinkwrapped, he made snow-Supers in the semi-fluffy snow. With no limbs, he swished his head in the wings areas.

I watched him snow-sculpt and thought I could light-sculpt on the glistening white canvas. What truth am I trying to convey with my crafted light? What forms do I want to capture in light? Against a white background do I blend or colorize?

I tried my candles on some evergreens. I placed my finials on limb tips or treetops. My light-flowers brightened the tree bases, ringing them like like their internal rings. I even tried my light-pillars from my El Arco Iris props.

Jettison and I worked side by side on our projects. He was tossing words around and I was tossing light. Being in the open air with a view of the cosmos was our version of Valhalla. Varuna and Vanir. Maybe the benevolent protector Vretil?

I pulsed material on Tree Cults like the Druids with an entire alphabet for divination based on trees and shrubs. The Scandinavian mighty ash tree Yagdrasil. Greek dedicated Poseidon the ash. Romans liked birches. Celts like the rowan. Hawthorne. Oak cults.

Some people believe Supernatural beings haunt trees. We know they visit and converse. Styrians had Vilyahs. French had Vertes. Good v names. Scandinavians had the horribly sounding Skogsnufvar. Macedonians called them Dryads. Welsh thought (another difficult sounding bunch) Gwragodd Annwn went into underwater palaces. The Firvulag and Tanu are shape-shifters. They are masters of illusion, farsense.

The Pulse records legends of Asar, Avalon, the Elysian Fields, Ratmansh, Ultima Thule, Agharta, Emhain, The Cloudlands. All kinds of illusion spinners. Bogle. Oh a v! Vanda-jo. Vough.

Since we categorize Supers basically into three groups: Supernals, Superlights, Superstars, we are not privy to all the names they secretly call themselves. People, Rainbows and Supernaturals identify Supers differently. It gets confusing.

Jettison and I looked at the noctilucent clouds. There's bioluminescence and Super and Rainbow luminescence lurking in these wild areas. We were in an area mostly inhabited by Supers, but in the Cascades there are Rainbow companies as well as Super-Rainbow companies.

Moonshine and sunshine illuminate the snow. My attempts at light-sculpture pale, but add to the lighting in my small way. The lightening points have vanished. How long would my light-sculptures last? Would they be considered light pollution? Light litter?

The Pulse says the universe is more dark matter and dark energy than light. Rainbows create light physically and metaphorically. I am trying to create a light thing of beauty.

On the mountain I feel closer to the cosmos. Closer to enlightenment and stellar energies. Mountains attract those of mystical bent, the recluse, the traveler. We transcend the profane and attempt truthful purity. Mountains are sacred to many people. I want to steer clear of anyone's sacred space.

Once I get my artistic vision clear, I'd like to go mountain-hopping globally. I could visit Albedo. Land on top of the highest peaks without worry about breath or climbing up. The winds may bounce me about, but wow what a ride! Wow, what a view! We really do not have many Rainbows in mountains. I'll be a pioneer.

On a mountain top close to universal energies, away from the crowds, away from the fluorescent energies within people, the sign and signal lights, the streetlights. Maybe I can draw starlight into my light-sculptures.

On a mountaintop the sun and star light are not artificial light sources. Here there are no campfire lights and hopefully no forest fires. Jettison and I, cocooned from the elements, can draw inspiration from the Pulse, the environment, the cosmos, from within us.

Snowfall slides or bounces off our Wrapps. We sidle up beside each other and roll over to a protected rocky overhang to keep our vision clear. Without boundaries, I can contemplate my life.

This is my first life. How can I live it best? Am I the everlasting candle whose wick is slow to burn out or the fast-flame easily doused?

30

The Letter V Is Like Two Peaks Beside a Valley

Jettison and I spent a lot of time defining our identities. Who really were we? What are we really supposed to do this First Life? What if this first life continues eternally on this planet with no change of form or location? Before we went urban, we'd better get more informed.

Hoodoo, down to Sisters up to the Three Sisters—Faith, Hope and Charity or North, Middle and South. Up and down, peak to peak. We decided to camp out eventually on the Middle Sister. Cuddled in a craggy alcove, protected from the storms, we explored the Pulse and ourselves. Snow blanketed. No need for a light-quilt. Snow tucked us in. In our Wrapps we were safe to explore.

While surfing the waves of the Pulse for my Waves, I decided to seek out V groups of Supernaturals. The v part of my name could use expansion. I admire the shape-shifters adept handling of light and density. I wanted to know some of the V groups.

In Norway there are sprites known as Vardogl, Vardygr, Vardivil and Vardoiel, who are luck-bearing beings to the person born with a caul. I could consider my Wrapps a caul. I could use a lucky sprite.

Norway also have Vaettir and at Faroe Island the Vattar, but they are house sprites. Wouldn't want them sharing my Wrapps. I'm not a horse Pulstar.

The v-names are so harsh. Pillywiggins are flower sprites with a giggly happy-sounding name. I wouldn't add Vazila. Vazila, is a domovoy who cares for horses. My rural experience with horses was not a good one. I do not care for horses.

140

Verdandi are fate-spinning Moerae in Scandinavia. Vihans are Korred kin (not a very appealing bunch). The Vivani and Vivene protect the Alps. They tend mountain trees and meadows. Way-vivani (or Way-vivene) is not bad. A possibility.

The Vodyaniye also have forest folk relations, the Leshy, but prefer watery affiliations. The Vouivre is a French, diamond-protecting, winged snake elf who hangs around fountains. People allege the Supers instigated the Great Squirrel Migration from Vyatka, Russia. I'll pass on those v's.

Maybe more relevant to my current situation would be the Vily. They seem to congregate in Europe, especially the Baltic area. Vily wood spirits live in deep forests on mountains with craggy peaks. Like other Supers, they care for and protect their domain. They especially like fruit, nut, fir and beech trees.

Also called Vileniki or Vilenaci, they are adept at healing and magical arts. They can be Vila-women and Vila-horses (there are those horses again). Some are foxes and wolves. I'm a chess piece not a four-limbed creature. Trees can harbor a Vila. How would I tell? No, not Vily or any offshoots.

People say a Vila is born during a fine rain in summer when sunlight breaks into mini-rainbows on the tree branches. Maybe a rainbow connection? No still not quite right.

After much contemplation I decided to leave my name Way-V when radrodding and find my artistic name when I am closer to my Visualizations global tour. I haven't even gone urban yet. Who knows what I will pick up and drop off there?

We also explored the space telescope sites on the Internet. The space shots and theories excited us. Funny energy. Quintessence. Open or closed universe. The Big Chill. The Big Crunch. Electroweak force. String theory-loops. All the questions led to endless discussions between Jettison and me. All the cosmology arguments. Plenty of time to contemplate them.

The mountains are my castles. I like the updraft. I like conjuring and congealing energy for my Wrapps and shrinkwrapps. I like to quicken.

In the mountains we are beyond the need to test good against evil. We are harmonic. A positive life force. We wonder about the Pulstars in other galaxies. The Kuiper and asteroid belts. The stars recycled from old star stuff. The stardust from earlier stars. Quasars. Quasistellar objects. Are bright-centered galaxies powered by black holes? What about planetesimals for such small beings as Rainbows?

We recall the Local Group: Andromeda, Magellanic Clouds, Triangulum galaxy, the Milky Way. The cluster of 30 or more galaxies to choose from. Part of the Supercluster Virgo Cluster of 2000-plus galaxies. Virgo is a v-word. Way-Virgo? No, not local enough. Space is the high-wide frontier which we left to ground down.

From a mountain peak I can explore the universe and the micro-mini worlds on Earth. I could stay here and never leave, though I know I must. Mustn't I?

31

Varsity Vaulting

Jettison and I did some varsity, no Olympian, vaulting from mountain top to mountain top, up and down the volcanic Cascades. Mt. Rainier (and surrounding wilderness areas), Mt. St. Helens, Mt. Adams, Mt. Hood, Three Fingered Jack, Mt. Washington, Mt. Jefferson, Mt. Thielson, Newberry Crater and Paulina Lake, various buttes (Ringo, Mokst, Klawhop, Pilpil, Klone, Wampus, Amota, Taghum, Lowullo to name a few), smaller peaks. We hovered over lava cast forests and Surveyors Ice Cave (I did not venture in). We did a lot of stargazing. You think when you gaze.

Jettison and I gazed at the digital universe by space telescope pictures on the Pulse and just looking from our miniscule selves. I became fascinated with spirals in space. The spiral arms of galaxies grab my attention.

Two big spiral galaxies dominate in the Local Group: our current residence the Milky Way and Andromeda, a mecca for many Pulstars. NGC300 is also a spiral. M51=the Whirlpool. The Whirlpool Galaxy is a bone-white spiral brightening blue sky. I searched for armless spirals, barred spirals, elliptical and irregular spirals.

I studied flattened systems with a central bulge and sets of dusty, gas-laden, star-forming spiral arms. I watched the flow of light. Ring galaxies join arms to make circles. Barred spirals begin at ends of bright stars extending out from a central bulge.

Being armless (or functionally armless) I studied the armless spirals, edge-on spirals.

The Local Group is one of many compact clusters of galaxies. The nearest compact cluster is Sculptor Group or North

Polar Group. Sculptor Group, now I thought that was cool. I began to experiment with pinnacles for mountain peaks and gyres, elongated spirals, for my urban jaunt.

Of course I sought out Vega. I considered Way-vega for awhile. It is a bright, blue-white star in Lyra. But I decided I needed an Earth name, which left out Venus. I am currently a mountain-dweller in the Oregon Cascades preparing to journey on.

Jettison and I toured via Pulse to many of the great mountains in the world we hoped to visit: Elbert, Sawatch, Aconcagua, Andes, Alps, the Himalayas, Tumucumaque. All kinds of mountains, folded, faultblock, dome or volcanic like my beloved Cascades.

Mountains can be a little tricky to get to. Mountains need various ways to get through, fly or hover, trestle or tunnel, cross through passes or go around them. Think of all the gods-in-residence people placed in mountains!

We saw the before and after pictures of the granite-faced Old Man of the Mountain east of Cannon Mountain. This icon of independence to the people of New Hampshire crumbled. Jettison said poetry, folklore, photographers and artists tried to capture the essence of this mountain. Carved by glaciers maybe 30,000 years ago the Old Man faced a lot of changes. The only constant seems to be change.

Jettison and I flew near Nasnan, the home of Maraki Shiri and Kaiam Kaga by Wallowa Lake. Ice Age glaciers scooped out the lake and left two of the greatest glacial moraines rising 500 to 950 feet above the lake. The Nez Perce declared the east moraine sacred. The suburban housing is banned from there. Still, suburbs can encroach on parts of moraines if land use planning falters. Rainbows deal with abuse of land use, the refuse. We can't defuse the refuse in water. We retreated to Mt. Howard. The Blue Mountains are magnificent. I really do not want to leave the Cascades for skyscrapers.

Jettison and I camp in a cliff-hanger rock. I check out the Pleiades, the dipper of Taurus. Six are easy to see. The seventh needs better vision. Some claim about a dozen stars in the Pleiades. Hum. The rainbow is usually considered to have seven stripes in the spectrum and I am writing the twelvth Rainbow Chronicle. Karen said I should archive my Waves. Some symbolism here? Naw. Just hanging around Jettison too much and finding connections that probably are not there.

Dubhe and Merak, the Pointers at the end of the Big Dipper, are not pointing me to the Urban Gang yet. Jettison and I are still into poetic leaps and record-high vaults. The versifier and the vaunt-courier moving vaward.

32

Vertex of Vortex

After all my discoveries and explorations I reached the zenith of the whirlpool. My whirling thoughts swirled around the mountain to the top. I had my pinnacles. From the galactic spiral and mountain whirl I had my gyre design. My sculpture started like a galactic bulge, elongated upwards and wound like trails around a mountain.

I made pinnacles for mountains with a wider base like a cone. I made more of a spiral spire for my gyre for the city. Mini-skyscrapers. Once I perfected the spiral technique for pinnacles, I dabbled in color. Would the white be too glaring if the mountain was not snow-capped? Would it blend better with the snow?

In all our mountain leapings I left samples. I had no idea how long they would last. I experimented with heights. My magnetism struggled with swirling the spiraling and with lassoing the heights. With the coiling, whether coned or spiked, I reached one foot for pinnacles and two feet for gyres.

My star-pointers reached toward the cosmos. I wanted them to be beautiful, uplifting. Light-energy from lightening points in inaccessible places. Not dot—art.

I studied vortexes, portals that access multidimensional fields. Whirlwinds, powerful swirling forms of fourth dimensional archetypes, forces that pull beings out of their sense of self and place. I wanted to find cosmic consciousness and funnel balance and harmony to Earth. Maybe my spirals will take me there someday. Timeless connections may find their way through the light spirals from the cosmos to Earth.

The universe is expanding. More opportunities for sentient beings. Leftovers from dead stars recycle into new galaxies, stars and planets. Maybe someday I can check out newer, cooler, less gaseous atmospheres. Maybe another pinata pop will fill up other worlds or send assistance here. Many forces work in the universe: nuclear (works within atoms), electromagnetic (gives matter structure) and gravity. I'm not sure exactly what kind of energy helps me create my light sculptures.

I'm not sure how the various waves rise, swell, roll and undulate. But somehow the energy waves make my light sculptures move into shape and after they are shaped. I experimented with the pinnacles going up and down like a spring. Would they lope down the slope like a slinky? Can I attach them so they don't whisk away in the wind?

The Cascades became my sculpture gallery. Some pinnacles were in color. Some moved up and down, collapsing and thrusting toward the sky. Magnetism seemed to provide enough stick. The breeze and wind flow through them. It was hard not to feel vainglorious.

Jettison spiraled poems on some of the pinnacles. We were a team. His mind whirled new poems. Maybe they aren't the best poems in the universe, but they are his poems and his attempts at expressing his awe and appreciation for this first life.

When I am able to go global I want to see glaciers. I want to go to Alaska and see the Wrangells and the dynamic vitality of the wilderness.

How I love the u-shaped, ice-sculpted, glacier-scooped valleys. How I love the vast pristine wilderness. How I love the mountains. My pinnacles are my tribute.

I will continue to experiment. When I move urban, my gyres will light skyscrapers. But will I love buildings as well as the mountains?

33

Vincible Values

There are some values such as privacy and isolation that should be overcome some of the time. Jettison and I were having great explorations, but we were not sharing them. We had not entered our poems or light sculptures on the Pulse. We had not received any feedback on our work. We went the via media. We decided to visit a joynt.

On a snowpeak in the Cascades (we won't say which because we wouldn't want any people who might read this to go there) there is a cave joynt called Cloud Nine. The name is from Dante's Paradise, the ninth and highest heaven. Inhabitants are blissful because they are so near good. There is a feeling of elation and well-being. Well, we'll see how Jettison and I fare. Since it is on a mountain, how could I be anything but joyous. But Cloud Nine is cooped up in a cave, not my favorite environment.

The hosts are two starstruck Pulstars called Sid (Sidereus) and Gaspa. Sid specializes in snowflake designs for Wrapps exteriors. Occasionally he flashed designs on the cave walls for the guests to take with them. Sid entered a plastic superhero, cape and all. It suits him well.

Gaspa is a porcelain fairy collectible. Gaspa prefers cloud sculpture. She spends a lot of time in the clouds and pulses her cloud-sculpture designs below from her retreat, Cloudburst.

When she is at Cloud Nine, she invites Rainbows to some aerial joynts beginning to form like Nimbus 7, Stratus 7, Cirrus 7 and Cumulus 7. Supers have access to many dimensions, but share Cloudlet with Rainbows. For a creative retreat for Super-Rainbows there is Cloudland.

Cloud Nine is more a vacation spot. A place to perform and inform. A place to talk with others also on down time. There are out of the way areas for self-expression and stages for performers.

When we arrived Sid was about to introduce the entertainment program. Gaspa greeted arrivals and drew their attention to the schedule of events light-painted near the entry.

Jettison and I meandered to the staging area. Many song and dance routines, some performance readings, some skits. We watched and tried to find the good in the performances no matter how little we liked them. Others in the audience of nineteen were not so generous with their clapping or positive shouts.

Sid introduced Jettison. "Jettison, our interning Pulstar laureate, studied with Sylvianne, Maraki Shiri, Musard, Larkin and is en route to intern with Svetla. Let's welcome, Jettison."

Jettison blanched stark white to read a poem.

Poets

Poets have heads in clouds,
their feet stuck in the mud.
Poets branch into the sky
and root before they bud.

Poets reach far and wide.
Boundaries don't bind them.
Poets travel fantastically.
They like to skirt and hem.

Poets abstract concretely,
place all on the line.
Poets form uniquely,
free words or confine.

Poets feel intensely,
express their truth and joy,
bounce on life's rhythms,
tweak, tinker and toy.

Comments from the crowd. "And then what?" "Weak ending" "Predictable rhymes" "So what!" "Show not tell" "Needs reworking" "Revise or abandon it" "Maybe your next internship will do the trick." Jettison did not read another poem.

After that response, I was a bit intimidated to put on my light art show. Jettison came back to stand beside me. He didn't utter a word.

Sid the announcer introduced me. "Our Cascade Queen, Way-V comes with a light art show. She lassos light. Let's welcome the slinky, light Queen, Way-V!" My natural ivory wanted to darken.

I was here to show all my light tricks, the results of my art explorations, all my quests for expression with light. I was a light magician showing varieties of kinetic sculptures. I spun my pinnacles and gyres, my beacons of beauty and light art. I juggled light balls. I vined and snaked light then wound them into balls or spirals. For my finale, my candles, my finials, my pinwheel flowers, my pillars, my pinnacles and my gyres surrounded me on the stage. Then I gathered the light inward and left the stage bare.

Comments from the crowd: "Too gaudy" "Too bright" "Too gimmicky" "Light tricks, how tacky" "Too flashy" "Light litter" "Glad she didn't leave any behind to clutter the stage."

Jettison and I did not know how to respond. We had worked so hard on our art. These nineteen Rainbows did not like it. Without comment to each other Jettison and I decided to leave.

Jettison put away his poems deep within. I tucked in my light deeper. We needed to rethink. This was not the place to do it. We needed to get out in the open.

Gaspa was at the entrance greeting a small cluster of Pulstars. Gaspa said, "I do hope you'll visit the aerial joynts. They are really ethereal lofts."

"Thank you," I said. I thought, perhaps we'd get a better reception there.

But on a rock on the mountainside Jettison and I discussed our experience. We didn't need a aerial joynt, we needed a creative retreat. We needed to get the kinks and glitches out. We needed to re-vision. We decided to go to Cloudland.

34

Verify the Vow Voucher

Jettison and I needed to check our Pulses to get instructions how to access the aerial joynts and the creative retreat Cloudlands. Rainbow life-sparks make many leaps in and out of form. We were not sure the procedures here. Cloudlands might be in an uneven dimension. These are the zones for expressing creativity and freedom.

Rainbow life-sparks first animated Earthen forms. They activated bodies created by people's hands and machines in their own images. They were designed as toys and collectibles. These Earthens made of many materials were under surveillance until freed by the Hub, the First Liberation Movement started by Karen Harmony Rainbow.

People still can not know we are alive. Our Rainbow Chronicles left with Laura Larrabee tell our story, but she needs to give the disks to her friend Linda Varsell. Laura is a tad senile, so it is not certain when that will be. We count on the delay in a way, but now with any activated Rainbows under Wrapps and protected by invisibility, they could not find us. I can write my Waves without fear of discovery.

Rainbow life-sparks had many restrictions and rules provided by the universe to protect them. Rainbow life-sparks released from their forms went to the Dream Dimension. Thought-forms of lighter density allowed Rainbows to create Zoion experiments and to plan the emigration of Rainbow life-sparks to LightHome to embody in orbs.

On Earth, for the Zoion experiment, bonded pairs created mid-density Spectrals and Changels to convey the liberation opportunity to Rainbows outside people's vision range. Spectrals were progeny of unwinged Rainbow progenitors. Changels had winged, usually angel, Rainbow progenitors. This is not available to us at present. We cannot create more Rainbow forms and most of the life-sparks involved are on LightHome.

Rainbow life-sparks can access other dimensions. Dream Heralds came back into Earthen form to share technology to release Rainbow life-sparks to LightHome. Cedar, Daisy Clem and Hugh were the Dream Heralds. On LightHome Dream Harbingers Jorden, Halcyon and Osmunda prepared the planet with instructions received in the Dream Dimension.

Rainbows (with Super assistance) were able to ground Floaters who did not follow instructions properly to go through the portal to LightHome. One Floater Sylvianne ended up in the Super dimension of Poetica until rescued by Larkin and Googol.

Some Rainbow life-sparks dwell in the self-imposed virtual reality of Dreamland. Many stabiles did not want to be mobile in the Rainbow reality on Earth so they created their own reality.

Some Rainbows chose Sparkling. Sparklings release many Rainbows from immovable bodies. A loaner from the museum is placed head to head with the stabile body. The life-spark leaped to animate the loaner. The first body stayed in place. The newly activated body was free to be. Nashira Lani was our first Sparkling success.

The Museum stocks unoccupied bodies left when millions of Rainbows left for LightHome. Neoma and Pager, operating from the Rainbow Redoubt reclaimed many leftover Rainbows for active duty later for Sparklings.

These stiffened, lifeless forms came alive when the Pulstars arrived. After the Cosmic Pinata burst, Pulstars carried their life-spark across the Local Group and brought more nanos to make the Rainbow mission more possible. Rainbows relied on Cosmic Cousins and Supers for many of their technological advancements. Rainbows are part of the universal harmonic plan. The arts and radrodding are their methods of conveying harmony. They needed the help of the Supers with dance, music, energy engineering, communication and transportation breakthroughs. Gifts given returned Rainbows from LightHome allowed the Supers to go to their own planet Superior as well as share Earth. Some Supers went to their Other World Avalon.

Now Supers in their Slips and Rainbows in their Wrapps can enlighten this planet in their different ways. Rainbow Radrods and Ripplers need to find their own ways to contribute to the Rainbow Path. Which brings me back to Jettison and me. We need a creative retreat and light infusion for our Rippler aspect as a poet and sculptor. We need to get our chess pieces into play for a new game. We need to find a new way to move.

How high can our Wrapps take us? How durable are our shrinkwrapps in aerial elements? Gaspa did not look worse for wear from her jaunts to Cloudburst. Somehow Rainbows are creating aerial joynts and retreats. Do we eject our life-spark and create a thought-form to operate there?

Is it a white, misty world? Old people myths talk of a Many-colored land. Their vision of Emhain was of a place with no sadness like grief or sorrow, no bodily afflictions like death and disease, no uncontrollable weather in this gentle land of sweet music. Sounds like a Supernal realm.

Jettison and I just want to meet the muses in rarified air. No static. Safe and cosy in our Wrapps. We want to be cradled, cupped toward the cosmos, very high in an esoteric, self-selected group.

I researched V fantasy places: Valinor, Vemish, Valley of Voe. What vaporous view can we expect at Cloudlands? No previews available on the Pulse. Cloudlands is, in part, each Rainbow's invention.

We learned we could travel to Cloudland in Wrapps. We could operate in Wrapps or shrinkwrapps. The aerial joynts were closer. There was a dimensional shift to enter Cloudlands. We had some energy adaptations to make. But we would not reduce to a life-spark or disintegrate to integrate later. Some of the nanos technology that also made Mazel, Beck and their close-clones possible?

We did not question how it was done, but how we could get there intact. Satisfied it seemed doable, we did it. We arrived at Cloudlands which looked cloud-like as we approached.

Standing inside a rainbow arch were two Rainbows of porcelain construction named Caela and Aston. Fragile bodies operated safely in the billowy surface. Birdsong from bluebirds twittering in and out of sight.

The pair were about an inch taller than Jettison and me. Both were more ornately attired. Aston was an archaic porcelain with the long-ponytail hair tied with a black bow at the neck (hair currently light-painted blue), ruffled shirt, vest and long coat (currently in tones of green), the tan tight pants clutched at the knee over long white socks and buckled shoes.

Caela with the many-layered, poofy yellow skirt, green shirt with gold-laced bodice, green fluffy sleeves, golden upswept hair flounced on top of her head was a picture of old-fashioned people fashion. But then Pulstars can't be picky about their forms. They take what is available. Pulstars can't all be chess queens.

After all the introduction, Jettison and I were asked questions. Caela asked if we wanted separate or shared area accommodations. Aston explained many creative Rainbows prefer to associate with writers or artists working on similar approaches.

We had interviews with Caela and Aston so they could have a better idea where to place us. First Caela asked Jettison why he came. Jettison shrinkwrapped and said, "I was told poetry is word play with image and sound. I'm not sure how to juggle them yet, but I want to try. I want to see how words line up."

"Just practice. Study some of the forms and invent your own nonce patterns. Each poem seeks its own structure. The more structures you know, the better chance for a fit. You might benefit from some workshops and critique sessions. Consult the Pulse for place. The gatherings are on-going," Caela suggested.

Then Aston asked me why I came. I explained, "I want to make beautiful light-sculptures that extend not offend the landscape."

Aston's mask-like face did not reveal the puzzlement in his voice. "We have cloud sculptors, dust sculptors, animators of stories with images and sound to appear on the Pulse and in joynts. Light-projectors yes. Light-sculptors no. You might consult with them, however, how to craft your light. Artists have critique groups and workshops. Consult the Pulse. The Pulse works here as well. However, most creators turn it off while musing here."

To start, Jettison and I agreed to work separately with writers and artists. We would not turn off our Pulse so we could convene and check in at some point. We had no idea how time worked here and how long we could stay.

We did Pulse headquarters where we were headed. We were to pick up our urban rotations right after our return. The first urban gangs had been deployed with the Bod-Prod. Whatever time system we returned from and to would have to do.

Jettison and I headed for different billows and differing cloudy areas. We worked on our art in our own ways. I huddled inside Wrapps when thinking. I light-painted scenes on cloud sculpted areas for my light-sculpting experiments. I enjoyed cloud-sculpting, but it would not transfer to ground.

As I was tossing light about, Jettison pulsed me. "I am ignoring the variorum at Cloud Nine. I am playing with V's, vaporing in your honor, Way-V."

"How's it working?" I asked.

He responded with the poem "My Way V."

I am a verser, I versify verse
   with volta or vowel rhyme,
      try verse drama and verse paragraph.

I am a versifier, verselibrist, visionary.
   I am versicular with vision and view,
      voice and value.

No verbless poetry
No vague vocabulary
No villanelle, villancico
verso tronco, verso sdrucciolo,
verso piano, versi sciolti or vers de societe
verus politicus, versus pythias,
versus spondaicus,
versicle, vignette, verset.

Yes vers libre, virelay, vorticism,
versification of versimilitude.

"What? Sounds vague to me. Very telly and overkill with the v's. It has sound, sense, but no passion," I suggested.

"O.k. I'll loosen the laces. I'll be in Pulse. Impulse. I'll work on that too."

Jettison and I worked for I have no idea how long. Our progress was hard to evaluate away from our stomping, playing fields. During one Pulse conversation, we decided it was time to go back to the mountains to retry our crafts.

The bluebird birdsong was not soothing to me. Bluebirds wove within my gyres and pinnacles and landed on my pinwheeling flowers. I didn't focus on candles or finials. They perched and chirped, singing in cosmic. My cosmic seemed in remission at this time, having used Global and English once Earth bound. If they were offering any constructive critiques, I missed most of it.

The bluebirds seemed to like the kinetic sculptures and muted colors. What Earth creatures preferred would have to wait. I had to decide on my statements and my methods. I had to please myself.

Jettison and I had our exit interviews with Aston and Caela. Both were in a scarlet phase at that moment. Their Pulstar assignment was to Cloudlands. In2it consulted with them to create a creative retreat at Cloudlands and with Shergotty and Shebang for overall planning in Solara while in transit. All four were in their assignments for the long haul. No rotations planned. They chose this Rainbow service.

In2it did cover the bases quite well and delivered the nanos. Now it was time for Jettison and me to ripple our arts. Jettison's radrod rotation would have to wait until after his internship with Sveltla. My Rippler/Radrod balance was about to teeter toward Radrod.

In Cloudlands while Jettison padded and pruned his poems, I experimented with size, density and intensity for my light-sculptures. They should draw attention, yet not be intrusive. I wanted them to be beautiful.

I would have to return to Earth to see if my new concepts fit the different environments they were intended for. Then I can pulse the ideas to the Pulse for others to try. I have not perfected all the light techniques yet.

But I need to test my theories on the Earth's environment not in some bluebird infested paradise moldable to my will. Caela and Aston accepted our departure with grace and gave us their best wishes.

The bluebirds' birdsong wafted from the cloudbank as Jettison and I headed back to the mountains, to the Oregon Cascades, to Mt. Bachelor, to a vug.

35

Vigil at the Vug

Coming down from such a lofty plane to the mundane required adjustments. We felt weightless there and weighted down here. But we landed safely and on target on our preselected mountain. We checked maps for a vug on Mt. Bachelor. Jettison and I discussed our creations and our destinations.

Jettison and I want to create something that doesn't exist now or before in our chosen media. Each sentient being has to decide how to live and how a participate, whether to help or harm. Jettison and I choose to help as Ripplers and Radrods. The balance is still a bit uneven.

Jettison and I head for different destinations. As we made preparation for departures, I said,"We are valorous variers on vagarious voyages."

"That may be so," Jettison replied. "but I'm sure we are late."

Jettison left first to join Svetla. We were actually going to miss each other. Bad poetry and a very strange-shaped pawn...I would miss the companionship. Pulsing is not the same as being together. We planned a Visualizations, global tour after this upcoming rotation before he left. We complemented each other.

As he floated away in Trope, I inflated Check and settled in a vug. I had a few tests to make and a few grounded light experiments to try. I will not be swallowed by snow in this rocky outcropping vug. I keep my light vigil for a little longer. The city can wait. Too many inhabitants there already.

In my small, unfilled rock cavity, I stargazed and twiddled with light. I fiddled with height, density, intensity. I adapted light-sculptures to locations. Cities could handle brighter lighting. Dimmer blending with the landscape would be best for my votive candles, my vaunty finials, my vectored pin-wheels and my vaulting pillars. My vortexing pinnacles can reflect star, sun and moonlight for an extra dazzle on mountaintops. My vertexing gyres will reflect artificial light.

I came to call my sculptured light, wholites. They are completely or wholely, wholly of light. Some are similar to holograms. I can create them for Quads, companies, joynts, museums as well as mountains and other places I visit.

My holites (shortened the word soon after) have an event horizon, a boundary around which nothing can escape. The shape and light remain intact. Longevity is unknown. But I have created something new. Holites exist and were invented by a Pulstar chess queen.

I pulsed my news to the Pulse. Global Pulsings expressed appreciation and interest in my samples. Neoma and Pager from the Rainbow Redoubt thought the holites would be beacons and like lighthouses despite their diminutive forms. They looked forward to encountering them on their rescue and recovery missions.

Jettison relayed his congratulations. Albedo invited me to the EER cluster in the Amazon. Onterra said she and Hugh look forward to seeing them on their journeys.

Everyone was warned that my earlier attempts may still be around, too big, too garish, too inappropriate. But Rain-bows took the news as part of the creative process. The light-ening points were gone. They didn't mind a few light-re-minders around. How many light-drops could I have left so early in my first life?

Angelyn and Nathane, Mazel and Beck sent messages. Also a reminder that my urban rotation was overdue. Angelyn and Nathane were orienting an urban gang in Port-land—next sunrise.

I carefully sculpted a farewell pinnacle. I leave my light skyscrapers before joining more solid ones. I end this Wave-let with intense excitement. Reluctantly I inflate Check to check in for orientation in Portland within view of Mt. Hood.

VI.

Indigo: Hope

Urban Gangs

Litter and Graffiti: Svetla Rippler Rainbow

Loud urban noises. Buildings jut tall.
So many levels. So many floors.
City choices. Dash and crawl.
So many walls. So many doors.

So many levels. So many floors.
People rush. Glass shines.
So many walls. So many doors.
Traffic jams. Air quality declines.

People rush. Glass shines.
Green patches. Window boxes.
Traffic jams. Air quality declines.
Grilled, barred entries. Locks.

Green patches, window boxes
enliven the breathing space.
Grilled, barred entries, locks
limit access in a crowded place.

Enliven the breathing space!
City choices! Dash and crawl
limit access in a crowded place.
Loud urban noises. Buildings jut tall.

36

Venting Vested Interest in Vexing Vicinity

Was I ready to leave the serenity of the mountains for the vicissitudes of the city? As I flew over Mt. Hood to enter Portland, it was late night. The sparkling lights of the city lured me downtown. I think I will like being in an urban gang and leaving my holites about. Portland is beautiful. The Columbia and Willamette rivers are wide and wonderful. Above me airplanes, below me barges.

The skyscrapers are not as high as some cities I've seen on the Pulse, but plenty high for me. I swooped by to glimpse the large sculpture Portlandia. I wished I dared enter the Portland Art Museum to see more art.

I swooped over the city as the sun rose getting a scoop on the city. Power towers. Under the street, lines energize people. Lightening points will enhance the energy flow. Max, rapid transit, buses, trains, vehicles of many sorts snort across the city making noise and air pollution. Streetlights, headlights, signs add to light pollution. Makes seeing stars more difficult.

I joined other Pulstars about to be oriented into an urban gang. We met in Portland's classical, Ming-style, Chinese garden: Lan Su Yuan (Garden of Awakening Orchids).

From the Pulse I learned of a quote from Wen Zhengming (1470-1557) "Most cherished in this mundane world is a place without traffic; truly in the midst of the city, there can be mountains and forests." Wow. Mountains.

Portland's Chinese sister city Suzhou is known for exquisite gardens. This walled city block is filled with nine buildings, 500 plants, 500 tons of stone from Suzhou, China. Pavilions, rocks, stones, 100 kinds of trees, bamboo, many plants: water plants, orchids, jasmine, wintersweet; serpentine

walkways, mosaic stone paths, a bridge over a large pond—
an urban oasis.

The garden's design concept was for harmony and tran-
quility. The yin and yang duality balanced with harmonic
results here. Jettison would love the poetry—couplets that
interplay with nature. Great start for our urban mission goals.

The Pulse proclaimed the garden purported "infinite
wonders of the universe within a limited urban space." A
perfect place for Pulstars to explore this organic whole com-
bination of plants, water, stone, architecture and poetry.

We were to meet at the Taihu rocks which frame a water-
fall. They symbolize high mountain peaks. About fourteen
Pulstars would fan out from the Portland area. We studied
our Bod-Prod enhanced lightening points patterns. Soon
Angelyn and Nathane arrived for the orientation. We were
waiting on stone before tackling pavement.

Angelyn and Nathane worked with Beck in Solara, but
with Beck's upgrades, they were able to travel more. They
have gone globally to orient Pulstars. They also train Pulstars
to orient Pulstars. Not all Rainbows are in the cities yet. Some
share less populated areas with Supers, as long as they are
not organic gardens.

I wasn't exactly the vanguard in the city. Portland was
just a launching pad for Seattle. I could plod my Bod-Prod
here before heading north. Portland looked like a pleasant
city: hills, waterfront, some attractive skyscrapers, apart-
ments and houses, museums, performance halls, parks. Rain.
Rain. Rain.

Angelyn and Nathane tried to get our attention from the
Pulse. We tuned in to them. They gave us some tips. Angelyn
presented:

Ground Rules for Urban Areas

1. Hover above the highest traffic. Remember people are
   different heights. Aim high. Trucks are taller than
   cars. Aim higher.

2. Don't enter or hit buildings or glass.

3. Use Bod-Prod intensity for all pavement. Less intensity for parks. Adjust accordingly.

4. Don't shrinkwrapp at ground level. You may need a quick getaway. You can shrinkwrapp on most roof tops. Ecoroofs are great campgrounds. Portland has several greening experiments.

5. Use auto-pilot when radrodding to keep on pattern and to avoid collisions.

6. Stop, look and listen before you use your Pulse. You need to pay full attention in an urban environment.

7. Don't pester pets, people or untamed animals. Leave zoo animals to Super care.

Nathane advised, "You must be alert and vigilant when working in the city. Nothing tilts Radrods into Ripplers faster than being part of an urban gang. We tend to cluster Radrods into gangs in cities for support and companionship. We are limited in available Pulstars at the moment. The work is harder here. The Pacific Northwest urban gang will have to support each other by Pulse. We can't even encourage pairing. You can see companions at joynts during down times. I'm sorry, you are on your own in the big city."

Angelyn added, "Get acquainted with the fourteen in this Pacific Northwest urban gang covering coastal cities. Exchange Pulse access information so you can keep in Pulse. Neoma and Pager receive most of their emergency calls from cities. They have trained teams to aid other Quads as well. The biggest dangers are at ground level. You must watch out for animals and people. Cities tend to bunch up and crowd creatures into paved areas and confined places. Many feel caged and snarly. Even though you are invisible, you can be destroyed if clutched, trampled or caught."

Nathane gave some emergency information. "If your form is punctured or damaged in anyway releasing your life-spark, you must use part of the body to Pulse emergency help. Hover your life-spark near the location where the accident occurred. Floater technology will allow you to enter a form brought to you from the museum. The Flock carries forms with aid workers quite promptly, but you may have to float about a bit, much like your cosmic travel mode. If necessary, rescue crews will have to remove your remains for disposal. People might not notice the damage they caused. Animals will find you inedible and trash you. Stay away from fire. If you cannot call the Pulse before leaving your body, head for the Rainbow Museum for replacement and obtain a new stiff to animate."

Despite my limbless state, I was a chess queen and proud of it. I intended to remain intact. Maybe something in my composition helped me focus light into holites. I'd like to continue to play the Radrod/Rippler game in this body.

Angelyn added, "If you like these gardens, check out the Japanese Gardens, another haven of tranquillity in Washington Park and the three public Rose Gardens.

I didn't stick around to get acquainted with the other members of my urban gang. I kept in Pulse with Jettison, Onterra and Albedo. I didn't plan any risky endeavors. I just would follow and adapt the patterns and leave holites about. It did not look like I would encounter people, animals or buildings if I was vigilant. I did not want to live fearfully. I would be careful.

My radrod work in Portland was limited. I noticed tall, thin, long houses about fifteen feet wide. I explored and radrodded some neighborhoods. I pondered how the patterns would work with buildings in the way. I just visualized the buildings as mountains and placed pinnacles on them. I placed gyres at ground level. My little holites pale in the intensity of neon. I felt I could increase intensity here.

Sometimes I left a gyre at a lightening point especially in a small yard or park. If people could sense my gyres, they would trip over them in Pioneer Square. But my gyres re-form if nudged.

Sometimes I planted a few pinwheel flowers in a window box. I enjoyed popping about Portland. For Rainbows passing through I left vigils of peaceful candles and skyward-pointing finials. They perched on benches, billboards, trash container rims.

I planted my holites on parts of the bridges. From a distance my pinpricks of light reminded me of the farout stars. The arches on some bridges just begged to be light-painted rainbows. But I did not have the time or inclination to do it.

Rain brought shiny streets, slippery sidewalks and dribbles over my Wrapp. I'd shake off the raindrops and dribbles, but they returned. I was on auto-pilot with limited vision. My holite production lessened. Artificial lights take over.

The honking, sirens, chatter, shouting sounds of the city did not interrupt my silent, solitary work. I pulsed Jettison currently on tour with Svetla in Helsinki. She was broadening his perspective. It was down time and a poetry-producing jaunt for both.

Jettison pulsed from outside a museum, "Way-V, we definitely need to put Helsinki on our Visualizations tour. I want you to see it. I miss you."

I pulsed back, "I miss you too. You must see Portland. We are going to have quite a full global tour I think. I'm off to Seattle."

Jettison pulsed, "Solo?"

"Solo. The Queen is in her throne alone."

37

Vicissitudes of a Versatile Vaulter

Portland may be vexing to some vested interests, but not to me. Portland has lots of sprawl, but tries to fill in urban housing and has wonderful parks. Many suburbs feed into Portland. I liked the diversity of architecture, the gardens, the watery environment. I liked watching the traffic on the freeways which sometimes stopped traffic to a standstill. It was as if they had parked. I enjoy the cities' concrete canyons.

I enjoyed one of the oldest malls Lloyd Center. I flew in ovals, level to level. As people shopped for things Pulstars do not need, I admired the ingenuity and ways they met their needs.

Since Seattle is a bigger city, I expected more of the same. It is on Puget Sound—ocean. How dynamic! A busy waterfront. Loops and loops of freeways beaded with traffic. More people, more buildings to avoid. More leaps from rooftop to rooftop. More places to place holites.

From the Pulse I learned Radrods were streaming into Rehab Centers globally from the hazards and challenges of city life. Some Radrods set up roof refuges. Telephone wire dwellers confronted bickering birds.

Parking lots and garages emptied later at night. Radrods would cluster for meetings of their urban gangs. Stray animals in alleys, homeless people unsheltered in the streets, graffiti on walls, pollution-darkened walls and pealing paint were some of the issues. But the Radrods were helpless to help.

Some aspects of city living just did not appeal to Radrods. Some left for the EER. The Pulse carried stories of the urban expansion. I checked out the Seattle scene. I found a gathering of Radrods at a parking garage roof.

I spiraled up the ramps to the top of a parking garage to meet with a Radrod cluster, the Seattle urban gang. They planned a gripe-time and a song and dance time, a little down time until they could breakaway to a joynt or to another assignment. I listened to the complaints and observations. Most had practical plastic, light-painted bodies. They had actual urban experience.

One gang member said, "Have you been caught under a sensor water faucet? I went in an open door of a rest room. I looked around the faucet, when splash, my Wrapps was under a waterfall. Quite fun until a man came in. I made a quick dash out of there as soon as the door opened."

Another member added, "The scale in cities makes me feel so small and insignificant. I don't really care to help people create more light pollution in this city. I'd like to take my lightening points elsewhere."

Another member said, "Have you checked out the Space Needle? It's like taking a ride on the merry-go-round with a grand view."

The gang members spilled out advice one after the other.

"Don't mess with the fleshy ones. The fish market has all kinds of slimy sea creatures displayed."

"Have you seen the lifeless Earthens in vending machines? Small homies. Urban animals. Small heroes. None in there long enough to be pre-1992."

"Did you hear of the damaged Radrod, who blew away his cover when injured? He hovered over his unprotected body and had to hope any people who found him would think a child dropped him."

"The magnetism needed to glom onto buildings in a storm can make escape later a slow ordeal. Better to seek the underground. There is a good joynt there also."

"The Bod-Prod works well with most pavement. But we have to go around multi-level buildings. Our quilting has needed closer stitching in the cities than we expected due to increased energy demands. Bod-Prodding takes increased focus. I want more down time when I radrod in cities."

"Do you ever wonder about the smothered seed under pavement? Sidewalks and streets cover growing ground. Buildings block growth also. Rain has less green to nourish in cities. I miss the rural areas."

I could not stay silent. I loved the city. "But don't you love vaulting building to building? Don't you love the energy and pulse in the city? I love the lights, the blazing colors. Seattle has hills which remind me of mountains. Seattle has the sea, boats. Seattle has all kinds of nooks and crannies to explore."

The gang all looked at me. I was the newcomer to the group.

"Well, it is a high and mighty queen. Can't even ask her to dance for she has no loose arms," said a shrinkwrapped soldier.

"We've found many checkmate situations in cities. Hope you continue to have a good game here," said a more generous cowboy.

"Parking garages and tall building make excellent places for stargazing when you are not hooked on the clearer images on the Pulse," said an astronaut. "It rains a lot here so the Pulse gets a lot of use."

"Let's dance," a jointed, plastic, infant-aged Radrod shouted. "Celebrate the city!"

We dance on the flat garage top, the circle and spiral dances that don't need partners. Even the dances that involved holding hands, many danced without touching. The gang brightened up their light-paint. We tuned into the Pulse for the same song. We could have accessed it, our chorchestral ourselves, but we just celebrated song after song, dance after dance until the commuters came in to park.

38

Vanquish Vandalism

The cities caused challenges for Radrods. We could light-paint over graffiti, but that did not help what people see. Rainbow Radrod artists can't cover up all the people paintings. We do enjoy the murals, and to be honest I like graffiti on some trains and some walls. Adds some color to the city.

Onterra came on The Pulse. "The Polygon advises Radrods to leave graffiti alone and let people handle it any way they want. The way to vanguish vandalism is to encourage people to beautify their cities and provide good opportunities for people who live there so they can live in cities harmonically."

My holites hopefully help beautify the city. Unfortunately only Supers, Rainbows and animals can see them. Some on the Pulse consider them "Light-litter."

People and pets litter the city with their discards and waste. They have picker-uppers and cleaners, but never seem to keep up with the tossers. For fun I have plopped a pinnacle holite over a tissue, a finial on a bottle, and stuck a candle in a bottle. Tin cans can hold my pinwheel floral bouquets. They are transitory art, but fun to do, like an outdoor art show. When they are recycled or trashed, my light goes with them.

I rainbow-stripe the window bars people use to prevent theft. Some doors have elaborate protection. I don't go inside buildings so I won't be intruding.

People will have to take care of their cities themselves. We just boot up the energy grid. We watch sad children find damaged playground equipment. Schools have their mean-spirited alterations too. With so many people living so close together, they should realize how important it is to have wholesome, beautiful surroundings.

People's imagination helped them survive over the past attempts to create Homo Sapiens. People's imagination formed Rainbow lives. As their toy, art and collectible creations we give people beauty, play and an outlet for their affections. We spark their imaginations. We help them survive.

People created the marvelous designs for housing, business, transportation and entertainment which make cities exciting to me. I love the roar of trains, the honking cars, the hum of activity. I like to people-watch, so having an abundance of them in one place is exhilarating.

Skyscrapers remind me of my mountains. I can look toward Mt. Rainier, even fly by. I fly over the tangled traffic, the islands, the Space Needle, all of Seattle and the sea nearby. I like high places and expanding horizons.

My favorite tall building (522 feet) and old skyscraper (1914) is the white Smith Tower. People look at the city from the 35th floor observation deck. I glom at the tippy-top.

The Pulse shows painted pigs, cows, ducks and other inanimate animals creating whimsy and color as they "roam" city sidewalks. Some cities have artistic benches. Traveling Rainbow troops like Wings perform on the benches to small Radrod crowds. When the Pulse and archives record the shows, the audience vastly expands.

Rippler artists have abundant wall and glass space in cities to create their invisible-to-people art. Some are murals and mosaics. The city Rainbows see is different from what people see.

But I am here to radrod and to ripple my holites. We are having global problems with the Bod-Prod. It sometimes means going subterranean to get to the dirt. With basements and below the pavement levels, it can take a while to get beneath the pavement to the ground.

Radrods seek demolition sites and try to radrod there before the new buildings go up. Once we realized that much can be under a sidewalk or street, we had to go back to re-quilt.

According to the Pulse the Bod-Prod had trouble with rubble from terrorist attacks and war. Underground transit and tunnels left airspace between street level and dirt. The Science Center researches ways to make lightening points connect aerial and subterranean energies at the surface.

In Seattle with its underground and all the multi-level roads, radrodding had to re-work the patterns. Bod-Prods were not intense enough to bridge the gaps. We could go through about two feet of pavement. But we were having to burrow deeper into the underground to make a connection. Too thick concrete and air space made for fewer connections. The Science Center had no answers yet. Breathless doesn't come calling on cue.

I didn't think I could leave Seattle until Radrods in the area worked on the problem. Already we were having to stitch the light-quilt closer in the city. Obstacles made us veer from the pattern. So I pulsed the Seattle area Radrods to gather to discuss the problem on an unused houseboat in Puget Sound.

The boat was small, but plenty large for the four other Radrods who showed up. All were Pulstars for the Rainbows had not radrodded this area. We needed to work together to energize Seattle.

The tallest in the group, Gerda, is a rubber, adult stereotype with upswept blonde hair, red dress and shoes, no make-up, statuesque at 5 inches. She did not tend toward leader-ship. Gerda is a willing follower, not an innovator or leader.

Next at three and one-half inches was a beige plastic cowboy. His back was red. No coloring on face or costume. His name is Flint. Flint had a beige knob on his back that did not seem to operate anything. He also had openings in the head, feet and back which he thought might help him focus lightening points. He suggests we become like a totem pole and with the intensity of five Bod-Prods, the accumulative energies could increase our range.

Then at two and three-quarter inches was a child with a short sleeveless dress. She was all pink rubber with only two blue eyes and red lips. She wore a spiky crown that said Liberty. She carried an unlit torch and a slate that said Miss America. She took the name on her crown: Liberty.

Liberty thought each Radrod could hit the same spot and hope each blast increased the breakthrough. Liberty wanted to complete this rotation quickly. Rubber is well-adapted to the rain here. Still she wanted to move on. But as she said, "Maybe the pink slate means I will miss America when I go global."

Liberty and I were very different queens in very different games. She thought if we had to work all together on each spot, we would never get our quilting done.

Smallest at two and one-half inches was a plastic with moving arms and legs dressed as an infant with green shorts and sleeveless white top and green accents. Green eyes and brown hair. He called himself Bailly after the moon's walled plains or "fields of ruin." Bailly was not an optimist in urban environments. Bailly probably would bail from Earth at the first chance of his first life. But Bailly proved a good team member and tried all the experiments with us.

The task seemed enormous. We were not sure how many of our lightening points took. We began by reinforcing and re-stitching what we had done. We constructed simple white-light holite domes over the spots. Maybe they will help tamp the light.

Other times we totem-poled to see if the arrowed energy would target the energies to bullseye the surface. Shrinkwrapped against the rain, we lined up and tried to magnetize our energy inflows and draws. We monitored our ebbs and flows. Though it was slow and tedious, we thought it had the best chance of success.

We reported our experiments to the Science Center. More scientists were working on it. Our data would be tested. But despite the humungous work to be done, the five of us began to go our separate ways.

We gathered in a joynt after a hard day's work after months of radrodding. We were in Skidaddles.

Bailly was first to tell us of changed plans. "I've decided to join the Neophytes." I was disturbed because these were Radrods who chose to hang around the joynts instead of energizing the city.

"But Bailly," I said. "We need all the Radrods we can get."

Bailly whirled his arms like fan blades. "Posh the one world for all beings concept. We can't repair the destruction of others. Let people steward their part just as Supers and Rainbows do. I'll be doing no harm. I am leaving for a Neophyte group in Miami. I won't be far from Disney World."

Arguments from the group were to no avail. Bailly inflated his Wrapp and left.

Then Liberty revealed her plans. "I requested a transfer. I leave in a week for Bali. There were openings and I took one."

We could only congratulate her on her fulfilling her dreams of global travel. I wish my plans for my Visualization tour were forthcoming.

Flint admitted he had put in for a transfer also. "I am leaving in two days for assignment in the Middle East. My orientation will be in Cairo, then I will move into troubled areas in the region."

Flint looked forward to the challenge. He felt our experiments in Seattle would help him in his work.

"What about you, Way-V?" asked Gerda.

"I have a few loose ends here. I want to do more radrodding and more holite experiments. Maybe some visiting Radrods to the joynts will be able to help me. What about you, Gerda?" She was the only one of the group not announcing plans to leave beside me.

"Way-V, our experiments here are inconclusive. But I learned a lot. I prefer work in the suburbs. I learned just before I came here that I will work in Solara on a suburban task force. We still have boundary problems with Supers, but many pesticided lawns and gardens don't interest Supers.

Radrods need to fill in the gaps. The light-quilt does not need as close a stitch as the city or as loose a stitch as rural and wilderness area. It looks like Seattle is yours."

Those who remained, radrodded until they left. We danced and watched shows at the joynts and shared our dreams for the new locations.

When they all left, I went to an apartment rooftop to practice my holites. I pulsed Jettison, now in Mexico City. I was lonely, though buildings and creatures crowded around me. In the crowd, I was alone. A queen without her court.

39

Vamoose Vermin, Varmints and Villains

My game plan contains unexpected moves. Life in the city forces me too often into viciousness in the underground, too often into tussles on the ground level, too often into peril on rooftops.

Seattle built on seven hills with spectacular Cascades (with the awesome Mt. Rainier) to the east, the Olympic Mountains and sea to the west—is a wonderful city to me.

In Seattle the Rainbow joynts are in the Pioneer Square underground area. Early Seattle loggers skid giant Douglas Fir and cedar down the hills to the mills on "skid road" muddy streets toward the sea near here.

The town was called New York at first and built with wood. The 1889 fire enflamed the low land wooden buildings and wooden or sawdust sidewalks. The rats were roasted. No people died.

When they rebuilt with brick and stone buildings and concrete sidewalks, they rebuilt a more solid upgraded city. They elevated the streets eight feet and higher above the former ground level. Vehicles and people could fall off the street down to the new concrete sidewalks. So the builders put in some beams between road wall over sidewalk to the building. They built their buildings higher to meet the higher street level.

The former entrances were now underground. This area became storage for old lumber, machines, signs and other enterprises. One reason they needed to get on higher ground was for when the high tide came in, the toilets became fountains.

Rainbows built their joynts among spider webs, rusted equipment, dusty furniture, piles of discarded lumber. In the abandoned area, there are many nooks and crannies. Slanted, cracked sidewalks can be light-painted as backdrops for stages. Skylights with grids of purple glass brighten some areas. Over the skylights the pedestrians cast shadows.

I started to understand encounters beyond my grasp in the underground. Seattle's underground is a haven for tourists (of many species), Rainbows joynts and rodents.

Rainbow joynts are out of the people tourist areas, thus attractive to rats as well. These creatures are ominous to us. Rodents look large and very toothy. We look small and tasty to them. Since we are recent residents, some have not discovered we are inedible.

More joynt sessions have been forced into levitation by a rodent invasion. They have a vicious nature when it comes to Rainbows. We have to have lookouts at the entries to joynts.

Once I hovered over the tour guide who said rats used the overhead pipes for a monorail, kind of a freeway or high way. We experience them at ground level. But the area people go to is only three blocks of maybe 25 blocks of underground. Rainbow joynts are the off-tour area. The rats love our area.

The rats caused bubonic plague here once. To us they are a plague of different, dangerous sort. I experienced such an invasion. All the Rainbows went airborne out of rodent reach while we were watching an enchanting, clogging dance.

Some Rainbows in other attacks had to evacuate form when clamped in teeth. People seem the only animals unable to penetrate our invisibility. No second sight for people to see Rainbows, fortunately. Rodents see a quick snack. They pounce too quickly to evaluate our poor nutritional value.

In this joynt the lookout gave us enough warning to levitate. The joynt had a high enough ceiling to save us all. We hung out hanging in mid-air until the rodents decided to move on to easier targets. I did not notice them using the pipes, but then they were out of sight quickly. Sometimes cats come looking for a rat-snack.

Cats and dogs seem smarter about us. They are more likely to chase us for fun or mischievously toy with us. We keep our distance.

At ground level the traffic in feet and insects could be as dangerous as wheels. I steered clear of sidewalks and streets, but pocket parks, some alleys, some off the beaten path places received some of my holites.

My bug battles began with placing holites in grassy patches, trashy alleys, or between railroad ties. One group of bugs would not budge for a lightening point placement which I like to embellish with a holite. They deliberately marched right through them.

Mosquitoes love to poke their proboscises into my holites. Minor punctures, but annoying.

One group of ants filked a people song about them as they trashed my holite. They marched the patterns they sung and left my holite holey before it reconstructed itself.

> The ants go marching single file,
>> eating all they find worthwhile
>> Hurray! Hurray!

> The ants go marching double lines
>> yum, what our appetite undermines
>> Hurray! Hurray!

> The ants go marching three by three
>> on our frenzied, feeding spree
>> Hurray! Hurray!

> The ants go marching four by four
>> finding garbage cans to explore
>> Hurray! Hurray!

> The ants go marching five by five
>> searching for bites to eat alive
>> Hurray! Hurray!

The ants go marching six by six
creating our own matrix
Hurray! Hurray!

The ants go marching seven by seven
we don't choose to march by eleven
Hurray! Hurray!

The ants go marching eight by eight
we snatch food right off the plate
Hurray! Hurray!

The ants go marching nine by nine
we glow in the sunshine
Hurray! Hurray!

The ants go marching ten by ten
we are ready to start again
Hurray! Hurray!

The ants go marching round and round
on the surface and underground
Hurray! Hurray!

The ants go marching again and again
to shine in the sun and avoid rain
Hurray! Hurray!

On no, maybe they were ready to start again! I took off and left the holite to recover and holdfast against other intruders. I have to rinse bug-splats off Check in fountains time to time. This was just such an occasion.

People trample my holites unless they are carefully placed. I try to keep them out of their reach. But when placed on ground level in parks or squares, some people are bound to inadvertently squish them.

When I am stargazing on rooftops, some bungling, bumbling bird with poor night vision invariably beaks me then drops me when the birdbrain discovers I am inedible. I seem more protected in the mountains. Here I am high up, exposed for the picking.

Some v's are not good words to have to deal with. Violence encapsules the v's in this Wave. This is supposed to be a harmonic mission. I have to watch where I go in the city—no matter where I am.

40

Volleys in Vain

Once when I meandered my way, shrinkwrapped from visiting a joynt in the underground, I came upon a company all dressed in black with lightning on various parts of their plastic soldier bodies. The unloaded guns had lightning running down them.

I pulsed archives as I approached. Oh my, SCABS. We thought we picked them all off in a confrontation at Harmony House decades ago. Apparently caught in a time warp were members of the Society Committed Against Breathers. Their mission was to bug Breathers, mostly people. They shut down computers, pulled plugs, carried off one sock from unattended dryers in laundromats, squirted toothpaste tubes, spilled pet food, pulled off parts of rusted mufflers, hid dropped keys out of sight—just annoyed people and their pets any chance they got.

Long ago SCABS wanted to kidnap Karen, whose organizational skills helped the Hub flourish. Maybe Karen could assist them in their trickery. An invasion force came to Harmony House while the Larrabees were away to overpower the Rainbows there. But all the Rainbows in residence became light-painted Karen clones. They had no idea which one was Karen. A traitor, Elin, had shown SCABS Karen's face. Guilt-ridden Elin admitted her treachery, so the Rainbows knew in advance the SCABS were coming.

The Rainbows were cordial to the SCABS, but did not reveal their true identities. Even the Super Samara densified to suitable thickness and glamourized herself into an excellent Karen. She worked hard to keep her face immovable.

The SCABS decided to wait the siege out in Pink Haven, the pink plain in the attic which was home to the science center and was to be the resting place for the three forms of the Dream Heralds: Hugh, Daisy Clem and Cedar.

Living among the harmonic, cheerful Rainbows who shared parades, plays, music and dance with them transformed the SCABS. They discarded their lightning and donned Hubcaps.

But here I was venturing into a group of five belligerent SCABS. Before I knew it, all five surrounded me.

One said, "A chess queen. How quaint. Looks really old. What are you doing here?"

"I am a Rainbow Radrod on an urban rotation. I'm in my first life. This body is a loaner." I began to inflate my shrinkwrapp into Check in case I had to check out quickly.

"A what? What are you bubbling about you?" said another.

"You have not met any Radrods? No Pulstars from the Cosmic Pinata? Did you not get an invitation to go to LightHome?"

"What nonsense are you talking about? Grab her and make her talk," commanded another.

I levitated safely out of reach. I had more mobility if they could only zing, perhaps zig-zag. "I am in my Wrapp. Do you have access to the Pulse?"

"What are you talking about, Queenie? Pulses are in Breathers," another insisted.

"They are nanos, upgrades in communication and transportation. You must have had no contact with Rainbows for a long time."

"They could be real useful technology to bug Breathers," said a mini-mid-air SCAB.

"We are on a harmonic mission. We would not share the upgrades with non-Rainbows. You have not seen Rainbows coming into the underground lately?"

"Queenie, we haven't been hanging around Rainbows. Rainbows haven't been in the underground for decades. When SCAB members went to fetch Karen, they never

returned. Guess they didn't catch her," said a SCAB drop-
ping quietly in the dirt.

They needed a lesson in Rainbow past. I told them about
the Rainbow Chronicles and how we were now allied with
Supernaturals and lived the lives of Radrods and Ripplers
adding to universal harmony and stewardship. I don't know
how long I hung around tossing comments back and forth
in a vain effort for peace.

"What a rip-snorting fairy tale!"

"Very out there. Real spacey."

"You expect us to believe that story?"

"What other magic trick do you have up your plugged
up sleeve?"

"Rainbows never had this technology. You're a tricky
Supernatural."

"We don't kowtow to royalty."

"Your command is not our wish."

I pulsed emergency for instructions. The SCAB scoffed
at my (to them) outrageous ideas. Rainbows were newly re-
turned to Seattle. These SCABS had not left the Seattle area
except for a few suburbs in all these years. They had no ac-
cess to communication channels. They found talk of global,
interplanetary comments totally unbelievable.

The Pulse said perhaps training in the nanos would con-
vert them. "Or make their aims at annoying Breathers more
effective," I reminded Neoma, who joined in the discussion
from the Redoubt.

I didn't know if the SCAB heard my conversations from
inside Check. I had ballooned Check into an area I could pace
in my hovering scooting manner.

"We don't have cells to imprison them, Way-V. My crow
Coronis can't carry all of them if they are cantankerous. Lock-
ing them up in birds until we brainwash them into Rainbow
thinking will not work."

"Neoma, should I just abandon them? They are evil
Earthens."

"I really have no word about any SCABS left. Most non-Rainbow Earthens are in Dreamlanders or Dormants. Some Rainbows are not closely affiliated, but they don't have evil intent."

"Well, I have a very unenviable public relations job here, Neoma. They are leaping up at me like flames. Anyone else have a suggestion?"

Various Rainbows pulsed messages to me.

"Go higher."

"Lull them with lullabies."

"Show them the nanos they could use if they joined our cause. Instructions how to use them come with conversion."

"Drop a holite over them. Lighten them up."

"Try a Bod-Prod beam."

"Call in the Seattle urban gang to surround them. Get some back up."

I was not far from the joynt I left. I could send an SOS there and hope they come quickly and subdue the SCABS. I could not mollify them with words. SCABS wanted nanos only to be pesky with Breathers. My chorchestral talents are not the most attuned. I doubted a holite or Bod-Prod would transform them.

So I called in the gang at the joynt called The Rainshed. Soon twenty Wrapps hovered overhead and circled the SCABS like an igloo. Our Wrapps hardly dent from the dull guns.

Indoctrination with plenty of documentaries from the Pulse, projected on the Wrapps all around the SCABS. High-volumed texts with surround-sound eventually led to the SCABS healing. Breathers were not a priority anymore.

I made some holites for the celebration at the Rainshed. The lightning disappeared and rainbows took over. We had a very good show with the ceremony. Lots of performers in the audience the night they assisted in converting the SCABS into Radrods. They had a lot more to learn before any could become Ripplers.

"Hail, Hail the gang's all here," shouted a former SCAB.

Let's hope so, I thought. Hopefully no more disenchanted SCABS or EERS in other dark places. It made me more wary and more cautious. But I still liked to visit the joynts after a hard day or night radrodding. I liked to decorate the staging areas with my holites. They kind of brighten up the underground also.

41

Veto the Vicious Circle

Though I did go to the joynts for companionship, information and entertainment, most of my time was spent radrodding and experimenting with my holites.

My holites images projected to the Pulse evoked different responses. They were called my "Spotlights" "Noodle-doodles" "Gleaming ground cover" "Blight-blobs" "Garish-globs" "Gnarly-gobs" "Trip the light fantastic." Some Rainbows attempted to smash the holites. But holites recover. Light prevails. You take the scraps of life to light-quilt or light-art. If you are part of the problem, you can be part of the solution.

Urban gangs tend to be territorial. I invaded their turf with my holites. Replacements for the four who left arrived and did not want to work as a team. They thought there were too many holites around in Seattle. Glittery lights were plentiful.

I intend to go global so I decided to create new holite designs. My studio was an old factory soon to be gentrified into urban renewal housing. My magnetism for curving light. My focus to target art on walls. My desire to play with light and find new games to play. For all these interests, I sought new approaches.

On the Pulse I accessed material on "The Field" by Lynne Taggert who searched for the secret force in the universe. She talks about a network of energy, the physicists called The Zero Point Field. It sounded a lot like part of the energy grid the Supers maintained and Rainbows radrodded connections. The theory says human minds and bodies (and I suspect Rainbows' also) are not separate from their environment. Supers and Rainbows know this and act accordingly. The theory calls people bundles of pulsating power. The claim is people are connected to the furthest reaches in the cosmos through "waves of the grandest dimensions."

Pulstars, Rainbows and Supers have experienced this. I want to use these waves in my holites. Cosmic connections? Why of course. Creativity and collective unconscious connections. Yes.

The theory suggests this force can help heal. People need to attach, engage with this world. Albert Einstein said "The field is the only reality." I doubt he was thinking of us. But we are part of the wave. We are part of the connection.

With the extra energy boost the Bod-Prod provides, I decided to use it for crafting my holites. Some body materials conduct Bod-Prod energy better than others. Ivory seems well-suited for my purposes. All resonances, essences, vibrations from other wave lengths in other dimensions! To make us more aware of them would be wonderful. I love Gaia and the chance to play the games, not just good and evil, but games beyond individual desire.

Since life on this planet seems to spiral out of control and I like cosmic spirals, I decided to research spiral designs. I love the galactic spirals. I love the photon stars which generate spirals of light to capture other stars to create systems of stars in galaxies and keep the galaxies from rotation out of form.

On the Pulse I viewed spirals shooting out of the sun, Chiron the rainbow bridge, starwaves, sounds of circles moving into spirals, Chimera, the archetype of winged beings and spiritual highs. Is there a seventh dimension, lines of pure thought communication?

I am morphic attempting to morph light. All things are props. We can appreciate the beauty and enhance the harmony in this world by our actions. Chanting is supposed to increase harmony. I want to incorporate music into my light-sculptures.

I heard that in seventh dimension you hear the music of the spheres. There the sound of wind is birdsong and the bluebird is the symbol of clarity. It is an atmosphere of light-learning. Well, I remembered bluebirds in Cloudlands. I remember birds at Rainbow House, the Malheur and on roof-tops. I am of mixed-opinion about birds.

Since I am not in the seventh dimension, I have to deal with Earth birds and find my clarity in my holites. Within the dusty, brick and plaster walls at the abandoned factory I would research spirals and attempt to create my new versions of holites. My queen's loft. I called my castle, Valari— a name of balance and harmony.

Some spirals are concentric circles. They looked better as flat paintings. I covered part of a wall with color variations. Also some playful labyrinths we might puzzled out. I invented spiral game boards for play in companies and joynts.

I enjoyed spiral webbing designs. Some I overlayed over other light-paintings. Decorative motifs like the Maori whorls from fern inspirations, triple spirals from the old stones, spirals from ancient times suggested new ideas.

I worked on kinetic spiral sculptures incorporating involution (rolling up) and unwinding or evolution. I could proceed from the center outward or from the outside inward. I was like lassoing rope. The noodle-doodle comment could apply here.

I chose the rebirth connotation people put on spirals, not the spiral sinking into death. I have a more cosmic orientation, the relation to the celestial galaxies, the life force whether cosmic or microcosmic.

I created whirlpools, coiled serpents, scrolls, sigmas, conical shells, spiral oculi—the double twists on threshold stones. Some of my spiral staircases had multi-colored stairs.

Also I tried the mythical sacred spiral of the river Styx. The spiral led to an underground womb. Someone can re-emerge after seven turns through the nether sphere. Seven sounded so Rainbow. So I put all seven rainbow colors in that spiral.

The pillars with Ionic spirals on top, volutes, sceptres (found a sceptre of compassionate wisdom and illumination called vajre or dorje), lituus and walking sticks were not symbols of power, but spiraled linear art.

Pillars in a grouping could guide Rainbow spiral dances. Mandala patterns could suggest placing. Dancing the light, not tripping the light, fantastic.

Then I moved to double spirals. The spiraling snakes on caduceus suggest a balance of opposing princples. One snake was harmony and the other disharmony. I made some yin-yang motifs in varying colors on my art gallery wall. I experimented with movement from the center.

I experimented with expanding spirals like a nebula. I created contracted spirals like whirlpools or whirlwinds. I created ossified spirals like shells of sea creatures.

I tried the spiral headdress of the Egyptian god Thoth. Spiral related to power, but I returned quickly to my circular, maybe somewhat spiraled, queenly crown.

My clockwise-directed spiral was very creative, I thought. Destructive spirals twirl to the left I learned. I tried a double-spiraled merudanda. One spiral is solar and one is lunar around the axis mundi. My cosmic contribution.

The hurricane lead to my vortexes. The vortexes in wind, water or fire lead me to incorporate movement and color. My holites ascended and descended. They whirled the rotating energy of the universe. I tried to incorporate a whoosh sound, but I haven't be able to add sound yet. Would I create vertigo with some of my spirals?

People have so many meanings for the open, flowing line of the spiral. To them spirals have a mystical center. Spirals symbolize growth, fertility and waxing and waning moon phases. Spirals suggest the rhythm of their breath and life. Double helix is DNA structure. People have whorls on their fingertips.

Spirals like a labyrinth suggest a difficult path in or out. I had put my time in and I wanted out of here. I was prepared for my global Visualizations tour. I'd have to add

Carnwath in Scotland, Castle Archdall in Ulster, Gravinias in Moribihan, New Grange in Ireland, some temple in Malta and a neolithic example in Bacha, Sweden. Robert Smithson's environmental sculpture "Spiral Jetty" in the Great Salt Lake.

I kept in-pulse with Jettison. He wanted me to go to a joynt and share my work. I placed my creations on the Pulse. I headed to the underground to Skidaddles to display my new holites.

I flew high above a city I would miss, even though I am eager to leave. Above the highway Check readies to swoop into the underground. The city's myriad mini-lights shine like flowers in a meadow. I want to nuzzle among the blooms.

The cars and trucks come closer as I seek landing. The humps and bumps on the slick pavement glisten with rain. I steer among my urban mountains.

I glide by windows and doors closed by cold and for safety. I like to leave my holite candles on the window sills. I veer toward electric lights. Neon and bulbs glare. My help-less arms can't turn them on or off. I can only turn on holites.

I await landing to guide my glide. I am proud Radrods help energize the lidded ground beneath the pavement. The world has not been paved barren for long. Now the gaseous vehicles flow where perfumed wildflowers and fragrant crops once grew. I see a domesticated plant framed inside a window. It might be medicine, edible, decorative. I leave a beacon. A pinwheel flower whirling on the sill.

Traffic lighted fore and aft hunch along. Slick surfaces soften rough textures. An artificial smoothness wettens to reflect light. I can not sense the loss of the wild with my touch, but I can with my thoughts.

Hopefully I can go on my Visualizations tour soon to see other places and bring my light there. I see signs to places I don't want to go. After this holite show, it will be back to radrodding. I have had about as much time off rippling as my radrodding conscience can accept.

42

V is Hope

V is like two arms reaching toward the universe with hope. I do not have such upreaching arms, but I have hope. Jettison pulsed he finished his internship and was coming to read in Seattle. My favorite underground joynt had been rodent-free for months. They must have caught on we were not worth catching.

With all the light-painting and my holites on display around the audience area, the joynt we nicknamed Rats seemed less cavish. I had not seen Jettison except over Pulse for a long time.

When Jettison arrived, he was light-painted all in black. He looked like a storm cloud. He walked up to the stage without even saying hello to me. He introduced himself as Jett. With a jumping bounce Jett performed a cinquo string: Slam

Slam—
modern
poetry—
sport of spoken
word.

Slam—
bam-words
Olympics.
Verbal slugfests
rule!

Bam
wham, ham
flam, jamb, cram
alla kazam
slam!

Slam
shout, laugh
wriggle words.
Find rhythm, moves,
time.

Slam
offense!
Offensive
intense power
words.

Rock
stars of
poetry.
No word wimps
slam.

Poems
engage
resonate
for everyone—
YES!

Who was this dark, strange, assertive creature who approached me? Do I still know Jett? The audience jumped up and down and hooted. The next act had to settle down the crowd. This was a very different style for Jettison. Had the world traveler jettisoned his reticence?

Jettison lightened up to tan and said, "How did you like it? My new style."

"I am a bit startled. I think I can get used to it. Do you want to be called Jett?" I asked. I loosened my shrinkwrapps.

"That is a stage name. You can call me Jettison, whatever you prefer. I hope you can get used to me. I have come to see if you are ready to go on the global Visualizations tour we dreamed about. How are your holites coming?" Jettison feels ready to tour? Am I ready?

We hovered over to an alcove near a holite gyre. "My holites endured city life. They seem durable and I am ready to place them elsewhere. I am not sure how much longer this rotation is."

"My internships are over. I'd like to travel more and get more ideas for my poems. We do have free will on this planet. We did get to decide how much Rippler time we wanted. We can still radrod and ripple. Your rotation orientations are over. What do you think?"

I paused a moment thinking over my rotations, the evolution of the holites, the times with Jettison. I'd traveled solo so long. I belonged to gangs and other companies and clusters sporatically.

Jettison tried to fill the silence. "We could go to Solara and get permission from Karen and Jorden. Onterra pulsed she is in Solara for some planning meetings. Won't you come?"

"It would be good to get permission for our tour. Then we wouldn't be assigned any more patterns in different Quads, Jettison." I was confident. "Yes, we can make our own plans."

"I miss our time in the mountains. It would be wonderful to travel with you again, Way-V." Jettison peached.

"I missed you too, Jettison. We need to plan high places into our tour. Let's plot some lightening point places and then go to Solara with our plan."

Jettison agreed. We huddled under a tipped flower pot on a gardened apartment roof I spotted earlier. No bird-peckers today. We were under cover.

Jettison had many places he wanted to be included on our trip. So many places he wanted to show me. On the Pulse I had seen so many places I wanted to drop off a holite.

Soon it was time to leave the often soggy city for arid Solara. We made a firm commitment to our plans. We would live our Visualizations.

VII.

Violet: Redemption

Global Visualizations

Music of the Spheres: Ki Harmony Rainbow

Rainbows circle land and sky.
We lasso Earth's energies,
loop loopholes, connect light,
we create synergies.

In sync with cosmic harmonies,
in sync outside and in,
in sync with Gaia's rhythms,
we find music within.

Sing and dance Rainbows!
Redeem each silent, still one.
Restore sense to each sentient being.
Rainbow redemption has begun.

43

Valiant Voicer—
Vivifying Visionary

Jettison and I raced in Trope and Check toward Solara. We flew into the cave entrance on cruise control to avoid bumping into walls or inhabitants. En route swaths of color blurred by. We were speeding too fast to concentrate on the details.

We found our destination. We shrinkwrapped (do I need sed in shrinkwrappsed? I'll leave spelling to Jettison). After we reached the home of Jorden and Karen, we wanted to discuss our plans for a global visualization tour.

Hugh and Onterra sat with Karen and Jorden on the curved benches around the mushroom-shaped table in the courtyard. They were telling of their recent romps visiting Albedo and Dawna in the Amazon.

After all the welcomings, Jettison and I waited for our turn to speak. But before we could say a word, a glistening blue ball hovered above us and landed in our midst.

"Greetings from your Cosmic Cousin, Breathless. I'm here for a nano-second with new nano upgrades. You have done such a good job with the bod-prod in your lightening point efforts, the universe is coming within your reach. You are antennas to the universe.

At the Science Center Googol will receive the codes to communicate with: Superior the Supernatural planet with Hazelle and Regal Eagle Rowan as first contacts. First contacts with LightHome will be Max and Halcyon. Gosta Berling will represent the book characters on LibreFree. From the first Earthen experiment, now living on FreeFlow, your contact will be Gaianna.

Service to the Dream Dimension and Avalon with Skia and Waug coming soon. At some point the portals to many places of the universe will be available to your life-spark. You can relocate or just visit.

The universe could use more Rainbows. You have proven your dedication and harmonic intent. Should people default, unable to sustain themselves or the planet, I'll pass on your availability and capability to steward the planet.

Ah, Jorden a ball requires the least energy to hold it together, but my energy wad feels water-logged. With enhanced communication I'll visit more often without form. Earth tends to bog me down. But I risk a certain heaviness to lighten up with my friends."

"It is always wonderful to see or hear from you, Breathless. The Earth is the perfect place for Rainbows. The lightening points appear to hold. Thank you so much for the new nanos. We become true cosmic citizens," said Jorden. Jorden gently tapped the glowing globe.

"Rainbows open up lives and connections," said Karen, placing her hand on Jorden's. "The Hub remains true."

Breathless seems to shimmer with their touch. The sheen on the blue ball begins to dim. "Long live the light. Long live Rainbows." Breathless blipped out.

All with the same intent, Karen, Jorden, Hugh, Onterra, Jettison and I inflated our Wrapps and raced to the Science Center to see if the cosmic codes had been downloaded.

When we arrived, Beck and Mazeltov, Larkin and Googol, Strangelette and Damian and all the scientists were spinning in a spiral dance of joy and celebration. The six of us joined on the tail-end.

44

Visitor with Vita Verdict

After the ecstatic dance, Googol tuned into extraterrestrial sites. The images and sounds funneled over Pulse to all in the Rainbow spectrum which included our allies, the Supers. Strange and exotic landscapes, barren and lush filled with four-limbed forms like most of us. Creatures of our Rainbow past. Maybe someday we will find other Pulstar communities colonizing the Local Group. Maybe outside the Milky Way in another galaxy like Andromeda. What forms and paths have they taken?

Suddenly there was an energy surge, slurge or purge. The Pulse impulsed a spinning disk of rainbow-light on our Pulse. It was a special message from In2it which interlaced our lives with many other life forms. I stored each info bite for later contemplation.

This is In2it with a bulletin of greatest importance. With the recent nano upgrade, I can talk with you longer and directly through the Pulse. Now that you are connected to the universe, I can tell you, Rainbows are here to help fulfill the Whirling Rainbow prophecy of Native American people to bring a Fifth World of Peace from the Fourth World of Separation.

(This connected Earthlings, Earthens and Supernaturals in a common cause. We can join together and make harmony happen.)

We can all be the Whirling Rainbows of peace and equality. All of the creatures of Earth will nourish the planet

and live in harmony. The rainbow colors will unite with
all colors whirling together.

Rainbows whirl their colors through the sky, land light-
ening points, redeem, restore energy, connect light
and energy. Rainbows bring their power to color
the Good Red Road with the Rainbow Path.

Supers add their energetic, healing. Supers' shape-
shifting magic, their songs, their dances spiral with
others.

In Hopi and Navaho tradition Whirling Rainbow
Woman brings rain for crops of corn, squash and
beans to nourish people. She is a healer and sustainer of
the Earth.

(This would be awesome! Everyone would be rainbow-
inclined inside.)

The image of the whirling rainbow can help you remem-
ber the purpose for your Earth journey and what abili-
ties you have to share to create unity from separation, to
find your part to create wholeness, to explore your
rhythm to make waves of harmony.

From inside the whirling rainbow, send joy and inner-
peace into discord. The knowing traditions of the
Warriors of the Rainbow unite with Rainbows
and Supernaturals to create the Fifth World of Peace.

(This is what my holites try to do, leave a bit of joy, awe,
and light for the wounded world. Vortexes to draw harmony
in.)

Trust your vision and assist the whole with joy and love.
Discover the twelve cycles of truth of the Iroquois:

learning, honoring, accepting, observing, hearing, presenting, loving, serving, living, working, walking and being grateful for the truth.

(This coincides with the Pulstar choices before we came and after we arrived. It is easier to know than to live.)

How do you do this? Remove negativity and discord from your life. Use the whirling rainbow to encircle disharmony. Learn your lessons. Create beauty and joy. You have the ability to create unity. Be part of wholeness. Heal others and the Earth. Understand and hear all creatures. Learn from all lifeforms. Love nature. Admire beauty. Acknowledge the sacredness of all lifeforms. Recreate the Uniworld we all come from.

(These are worthy goals. These goals provide life-long challenges.)

Earth is the mother that birthed our bodies. Fire is our essence that comes from the stars. Each lifeform is part of the perfect whole created in unconditional love by the Great Mystery, Original Source, Omni-sparkler, Grand Designer, God or any name Earth-beings choose.

With compassion, mutual respect and love, round the full circle for all. Remain connected to the universal family of creation. When you travel the Blue Road of Spirit, you will have placed your life-piece into the harmonic puzzle of the Great Mystery, the Omni-Sparkler, Prime Creator.

As Whirling Rainbows you stir up remembering dreams of how to heal soil and water, to quicken awareness in people. A Sun Dog, full rainbow around the sun, will portend the Fifth World—the Time of the White Buffalo. All beings will be awakened to their respon - sibilities to heal each other and the planet. Rainbows and Supers are awakening before most people.

(This will make Supers happy. They received cosmic guidance before Rainbows and shared the gifts with us.)

Native Americans believe wind is a forerunner of lessons. From the south come teachings of trust, faith, innocence.

From the West comes inner-knowing, introspection on seeking answers and goals.

From the North acknowledge gratitude and wisdom.

From the East discover breakthroughs and new ideas.

Illumination brings freedom, new levels of understanding.

(Maybe some of these words can be on my illuminations, my holites. Maybe my spirals are images for the Whirling Rainbows.)

Forms may change, but the energy of creation is regenerative and eternal. A vibral core or primal energy source some call the Great Spirit or creative principal directs the creative flow of the Uniworld which connects all the universes, all levels of consciousness, all understanding and all life in cahoots with the Great Mystery. All lifeforms are part of this creative, light-unfolding, infinite, evolving, progressive creation.

(Maybe I will create new light-art for this swirling, unifying, energy.)

Lifeforms have free will to choose what path to take. All are part of the whole to contribute talents and beauty for the Uniworld. Each lifeform can contribute uniqueness toward harmony and truth. We are all co-creators with the Original Source. Light and lighten the flow. Make waves in rhythm with the Earth and reach out to the stars.

Pay attention to any lifeform speaking the language of love. Be willing to understand, feel, act. Open new doors of expression and expansion. Live to fulfill the prophecy for a Fifth World of Peace.

The disk swirled like a frisbee back to the cosmos. As I was enwrapped in my Wrapp, my global Visualizations tour seemed even more urgent and important. I wanted to make my points, create my art and do my part.

Everyone was ecstatic! The jumping and dancing began again. Supers and Rainbows celebrated for quite awhile until Googol suggested we look at the big Pulse screen at the science center to see what others far away were thinking.

We went back to viewing and connecting with lifeforms with a similar image. Part of my first life is learning about other lives who once lived on Earth and chose other domains.

In excitement the Rainbows watched the Pulse reach other destinations. Solarans clustered or alone in their Slips viewed the newest revelation.

On the big screen pulsed to all who cared to watch were Hazelle and Regal Eagle Rowan taking us on a tour of a lush planet, harmonized by creatures similar to the shape-shifters they were. Max and Halcyon report the orbs and blobs live in harmony with expressions of beauty and tolerance. Gaianna on Freeflow and Gosta on Librefree also report allegiance to the Whirling Rainbow concept. All hope the Earth attunes soon.

In the hurly-burly, circus atmosphere I did not have a chance to discuss my global Visualizations tour. Can I launch my artistic path globally? Did I complete my apprenticeship? Can I exert my free will?

Check floated me to a quiet spot where I could view the Pulse in private. This part of the cave was not light-painted or glamoured, just the natural cave wall waiting for my imprint.

I am in the West seeking through introspection answers and goals within the whirling rainbow. Can I create a flat whirling rainbow icon? My pinnacles and gyres already have the gist. I'd like to give it a twirl. This Rainbow would like to whirl worldwide.

45

Vital Signs and Velleity

My plans for discussing my game plan moves were delayed by an emergency meeting of the Polygon coordinated by the Octagon. Some of our Super allies were not inclined to join the Whirling Rainbow prophecy. The Polygon decided to gather a Super-Rainbow Council in the Super Sol Theater. Rainbows and Superlights had access to the meeting by Pulse.

Lithania greeted the guests in a culotte outfit. The orange background supported sequined flowers in silver. Her wings had silver accents as well. She contacted the Superstars in the Earth's core and the Supernals, the aerial variety often considered angels by people. The Supernaturals have three layers of being, often imagined as a sandwich. The bottom layer being the Superstars, the middle spread the Superlights and the top layer the Supernals. The Supernals and Superstars support the Whirling Rainbow concept. They were not concerned with the name. They wanted just the same role as before, making the same moves and flowing energy through the Rainbows to tie the lightening point. We are like straws drawing up and thrusting down the energy they provide.

But in the crunch of the munch are the Superlights. Their independent spirit did not want Rainbow in any prophecy or mission statement. It made no difference that some people had no problem with the rainbow idea. Of course Rainbows felt very pleased with the naming and the concept.

Jettison was encased in Trope writing a poem called Whirling Rainbows. I remained inside Check screening the proceedings. I did not want to interrupt Jettison's muse.

Would the whirling rainbow spiral out discord and center peace? Would Rainbows' inner peace and joy reach the Superlights?

When the elegant Superlights with their flowing gowns and blousing shirts and trousers spoke, I was entranced by their beauty. Their shape-shifting ability changed their light intensity, their density, their color preferences and their appearances. When disengaged they would go invisible.

Very visible were Googol, Larkin, Trella, Goolkin and Strangelette, Leanon, Sparrow, Samara with Ki. After many disputes, the Gentle Genius Googol, dressed in a tight-fitting, gold outfit with a whirling rainbow on his chest spoke, "Ever since I met Rainbows, I have aided their technological development. Samara aided the Western Network. Superlights taught Rainbows how to dance, to light-write, to compose music, to fly. The whirling rainbow is an image. All lifeforms belong to the rainbow spectrum of light and life."

His partner the poet Larkin wore a similar outfit—both dressed for a spaceship into the Local Group galaxies. She suggested each individual Superlight make a decision to work more closely with the Whirling Rainbow prophecy or interlace more loosely as an ally.

Pulse responses poured into the theater from Rainbows and Superlights. It seems like some Earthlings, some Earthens and some Supernaturals were not tuned into any cosmic destiny ideas.

As I huddled inside Check, I tuned out the debate. Since it was an individual decision for all, let them make it. With renewed vim and vigor, I flew out of Solara for an appreciative view of the desert. The beauty and the wonder of the world still amazes me. I swirled some ocotillos and placed some gyres on the top of saguaros. My holites surround the sharp points and glow in the setting sun.

46

Via Media: Viewing Visualizers' Verve

Each lifeform made a decision how to participate, or not. While the Octagon responded to the outpouring of ideas, I busied myself with placing holites in parks and planting pinwheel flowers in gardens. Theater entrances emboldened with my intricate new borders invited Solarans in to plays and other entertainments. While Jettison mused, I flittered about. Check flew rainbow streamers as we careened about the passageways. I practiced for my global Visualizations tour.

Check perched on a mushroom table in a highly sculptured and painted park. I pondered about the Whirling Rainbow prophecy. Will there ever be enough of us to serve and energize the whole Earth? All lifeforms need to sustain each other. A cosmic cataclysm could end it all for many here. We are privileged to have life now.

I still crave the high places. The urban pulse and city energy excite me. Mountains can be climbed anywhere.

I'm eager to get global. When Jettison finishes his poem and the media rush is over, I can present my plan. Rainbows and Supers seek contact with other planets. They discuss their role in the Whirling Rainbow prophecy. The Pulse beats fast. It is exhilerating so many connections are being made.

I decided to connect with a few of my friends. First I contacted Onterra. She is happy with Hugh surveying the South African veld.

Next I contacted Albedo. Contentedly, he is enjoying being King of the Jungle with Dawna. They will be part of the Whirling Rainbow protecting endangered species.

Then I contacted Burp/Rainbowlegged/Octavior and Marissa at Rainbow House. Burp calls himself Octavior now.

He is still vigilant over Laura. Laura is still perking along. Quite elderly, she is even more likely not to dust. Octavior and Marissa have his body for sparkling hidden under the house. Octavior has company and will become a Radrod when released from care for Laura. The Honeymooners moved away to live with Laura's granddaughter Rowan. Someday Harmony House is destined for a doll museum.

Nathane and Angelyn were in St. Petersburg flying through the Hermitage.

Daisy Clem and Amani were at Multnomah Falls watching the tourists (nearly number one tourist spot in Oregon). They hydroplane down the waterfall. "Quite a go with the flow moment, I would say," said Amani.

Nytanu has not perfected 3-D transmission, but he enjoys taking his global shots. He has a companion on his rounds now. She is also a photographer in training. Nytanu is trying to see how high off the ground he can shoot down from and how far he can telescope into the sky. He colors sky photos from space telescopes.

Trella and Goolkin took the twins to a joynt in Taos, New Mexico. The joynt had Native American motifs, whirling rainbows, drumming, dancing. Superlights and Rainbows could get in the whirl.

But I am stuck in Solara, buzzing about like a bee stinging light into darkened places. I am ready to move along to some enlightened places.

The scientists in the Science Center eagerly beamed the universe. Googol, Damian, Strangelette and Cedar projected seminars on their discoveries for others.

The entertainers with Wings, Maraki Shiri, dancers Osmunda (Oz), Lois joined the Body Electric: Leanon and Sparrow, Larkin, Ki and Samara in a production called "Whirling Rainbows"—a Super-Rainbow Production. If Jettison finishes his poem, it might become part of the production. I offered my Whirling Rainbow designs as backdrops and props.

Mazeltov and Beck collected and synthesized much new data. However, they took some down time to play computer games and attend performances in the many theaters in Solara. Their ingenious go-carts could carry them safely, handle any terrain. They often traveled holding hands.

I want to be a noun with a verb. Where will my next move take me?

47

Volte-face

My voltage was going too low if I did not do an about face. Time to consider a reversal in my plans. I wanted to be on the Whirling Rainbow Path. However, the road less traveled is probably not paved. Goals paved with good intentions may be covered over. Quad Four is not my horizon.

With Jettison tied up with the "Whirling Rainbow" pageant, Check and I decided to check out some potential light-drop stops. I pulsed Jettison a good-bye and good luck with the poems.

Off to look for the verisimilar and versicolor. Looking for plop spots. With Visualizations I wanted to preserve beauty before change. Places altered by weather, time, destruction by mining, drilling, logging etc. Find beautiful places impacted by people. I'll thought-carve my impressions and project my images. My in-pulsing can out-pulse on the Pulse.

I'm looking for motifs for holights—holographic sculptures. Reproduce and express light-filled images in new forms. I look for color and texture. Why not dust sculptures? Dust-flecked or solid light. Holights could be 3-D paintings. What imprint will I make on the world? The Zoion Experiments created light-forms that could host Rainbow life-sparks. Holights would not host life-sparks. Ideas, not life-sparks animate them.

I experimented with morphing visualizations and expanding my expression range. I had free will. I did not need permission to go on a whirlwind world tour. I will use all my rotation skills to become a diverse light-artist. Sculpting like a laser.

Check and I did not go global—Pacific rim and transcontinental USA. I visited doll museums in Bellevue, Washington, and Rochester, New York,to view our past. I viewed the animation techniques of filmmakers to imagine our future. I studied the post-1992 Earthens devoid of life, but still fascinating forms to ponder if they would ever experience a cosmic pinata burst that would enliven them. I light-painted a few to spruce up their appearance in case cosmic immigrants come calling.

I explored natural forms. Despite my aversion to caves, I ventured into Carlsbad Caverns, renown for beauty. The ranger sat the people visitors on a stone bench and warned them not to touch the formations, stay on the trail. No gum, food, racing or shouting.

None of the restrictions applied to me. Inside Check I could explore areas of the caverns still in the dark. I was my own flashlight and radar. In the Big Room formations had names like Rock of Ages or Painted Grotto. The Giant Dome is in the Big Room's Hall of Giants. The scale and distances are awesome.

Early visitors entered in buckets once used to mine bat guano. Today visitors walk on paved paths or descend in elevators. Check and I just went our own way. Being a Pulstar has some advantages in gigantic vastness. Audio messages guide all visitors. I was surprised to see a lunch room when the ranger warned no food in the cave.

Over 100 other caves are in the area. Many inaccessible to people. But with my self-propelled flashight I toured some caves to study the forms and beauty. The smaller scale appeals to me. Spider Cave and Hall of the White Giant admit few visitors at a time. I liked not having to worry about bumping into people by flying above them or around them.

Some of the caves have tight squeezes, flashlight and lantern illumination, dirt trails not asphalt. Vandalism closed some areas. Hundreds of thousands of Mexican freetail bats foray for food at dusk. Bats may return to the cave, but I probably will not. I'll create my light-sculptures on the surface.

I was most impressed by the treeless, volcanic crater Easter Island. The giant human statues. The mute sentinels. The Moai. Volcanic rocks on sacred platform sites. The natives expressed in stone. Left little oral tradition. The Moai elevated the spirit between earth and sky. Sixty-five tons of rock statue faces inland. Easter Island appears an ecological and social catastrophe, but the sculptures are magnificent. They are on a scale I can only dream of, but an inspiration to think big. People like to think big and build big.

We were built small, but we play the game of life with a huge spirit. I concluded this was too grand a scale for my light-touch and it was best in its natural state. But with my lightening points, I want to leave my light-sculpture. I'm a radrod-artist.

Reluctantly, I left the open space of Easter Island toward the cave of Solara. On auto-pilot I crossed the Pacific. I checked the Pulse for V's. I found stories, folktales from Russia and Baltic area of Vasalisa The Wise (or Wassilissa the Wise) or Vasilisa the Beautiful. One version was called The Doll in Her Pocket. Then I found a version from a doll's point of view written by Vidacita.

Vidacita in Her Pocket

Once there was and there was not an icon of intuition who called herself Vidacita. Vidacita was a tiny doll dressed in the same color code as the girl and three horsemen in the story: black, red and white.

Vidacita wore red boots, white apron, black skirt and an embroidered vest. A dying mother gave Vidacita to her daughter, Vasilisa. She told her daughter to keep "the doll" hidden in her pocket. If she fed the doll, the doll would guide her when she needed assistance in any situation.

In the story the doll was nameless, so the doll called herself Vidacita. This story is from pre-Rainbow times, so people's imagination invented that Vidacita could eat and jump around in the pocket and talk to Vasilisa. This is a revisionist view from Vidacita's point of view. Vidacita was bound to Vasilisa to get her out of binds.

After Vasilisa's mother's death, I found myself plunked in a pocket for service to Vasilisa. It was her dying wish that Vasilisa keep me hidden in her pocket. She was to nourish me and follow my homing instincts and wisdom.

Later Vasilisa's father remarried and left us with the stereotypical evil stepmother and two ugly stepsisters envious of Vasilisa's beauty.

Vasilisa's father went on a long trip, leaving her to work hard at her stepfamily's bidding. Vasilisa would feed me tender morsels and I would listen to her woes and help her out in this troubling, miserable, joyless situation. I provided her suntan lotion to protect her fair skin from the sun. With my help she led an easier life.

Suitors came for Vasilisa's hand, but the stepmother said the stepsisters had to be married off first. They moved to a house in the deep woods near the home of the legendary Baba Yaga.

One sister made lace. One sister knit stockings. Vasilisa spun. The mother was the supervisor. One night through trickery of the mother and sisters, the light went out. No one but Vasilisa was considered suitable to go through the deep, dark woods to seek light from their fearsome neighbor.

Vasilisa was sent to Baba Yaga for a light. The stepmother and stepsisters hoped Baba Yaga would eat Vasilisa. Inside Vasilisa's pocket I guided her on her way to the somewhat weird, witchy Baba Yaga.

The elderly, fierce Baba Yaga liked to fly in a cauldron steered by an oar shaped like a pestle. She broomed the air with her hair. Baba Yaga lived in a house that whirled about on tall chicken legs. The bolts on the doors and shutters were human fingers, human legs were doorposts, sharp teeth were the lock, human skulls fenced the yard. A tad intimidating.

She tended to eat someone if they did not treat her with respect.

I calmed Vasilisa and helped her with her words and actions in this fairy tale environment so she did not get devoured.

Baba Yaga said if Vasalisa would do some chores, she would give her light because she asked (apparently in a courteous fashion). Just like Vasilisa's stepfamily, Baba Yaga put Vasilisa to work. Vasilisa served and Baba Yaga ate a dinner meant for ten. Vasilisa shared the leftovers, meager pickings with me as her mother advised. Lots of concerns about nourishment and eating in this tale. From my perspective I was just the inner knowing Vasilisa needed to get through difficult trials.

Baba Yaga had a long wish list: wash clothes, sweep yard, clean house, prepare food, separate the mildewed corn from the good corn, keep things in order.

So I told Vasilisa to sleep and when the two gals woke up I had the chores done to perfection. The corn sorting was especially tedious. This was pre-Rainbow technology. I'm telling the tale now because I was passed on generation to generation from mother to daughter until finally I was freed to live my own life, my own inner knowing.

Baba Yaga was impressed with my prowess, so told Vasilisa she could do a few more tasks. If I thought corn plucking was tedious, poppy seed retrieval was worse. Baba Yaga wanted poppy seeds in a mound of dirt sorted so there was one pile of poppy seeds and one pile of dirt.

I reassured Vasilisa that this could be done. I did have enough magnetism to flow through my hands to extract the poppy seeds. Baba Yaga considered Vasilisa a lucky girl. Yes, because of me I might add. I was lucky that three pairs of unattached hands appeared to press the oil from the poppy seeds.

Vasilisa wanted to ask Baba Yaga some questions. I guided her so she would not become a Baba Yaga snack by stepping over the line. Vasilisa wanted to know about the three horsemen she saw.

Baba Yaga said the white horseman was her day, the red horseman the rising sun and the black horseman was night. The monochrome horses and horsemen vanished, galloping away.

Vasilisa was about to ask more questions when I jumped up and down to warn her it was not a good idea. Baba Yaga had said to her that to know too much can make one old too soon. If Vasilisa wanted to live to be old, she had better keep her mouth shut or be food for Baba Yaga's moving mouth.

Vasilisa was beautiful and not eager to age or stick around. When she said she came by the blessing of her mother (me), Baba Yaga sent her home with light—a skull filled with fire on a stick.

I warned Vasilisa to take the fire and go swiftly through the forest back to the stepmother and stepsisters with the light. No need to start a forest fire.

With my guidance she arrived safely. Things were not so good for the stepfamily. The skull burned them to ash. Vasilisa buried the skull in the yard.

The now homeless Vasilisa went to live with a childless, benevolent Old Woman. The Old Woman bought her flax to spin. Of course, I helped Vasilisa. I made her a wonderful loom while she slept.

With my help, Vasilisa wove fine linen. She told the Old Woman, whom she called Grandma just like she addressed Baba Yaga, to sell the cloth and keep the money for herself. I was just called doll and had no need for money. Glad to help out.

The Old Woman took the cloth to the tsar to offer as a gift. The tsar was so impressed he wanted shirts made out of the fine, bleached linen. He wanted to meet the needlewoman who created this cloth. Of course among royalty, dolls were given as gifts, as tokens of good will. But for this story, the tsar had to meet Vasilisa, not Vidacita.

So Vasilisa and I headed to meet the tsar. Of course in the fairy tale tradition, the tsar fell in love with this talented beauty and they married.

When the father finally returned, he joined the Old Woman to live with his daughter. I remained with Vasilisa helping her cope with her new role and better-financed, more leisurely circumstances.

Vasilisa gave me to her daughter. Mother to daughter I passed through many women's lives. None of the women could do their work without my help. Dolls provide mana, an inner knowing. The people-version of this story has been scoured for metaphor, symbolism and psychological insight.

From my point of view it reveals insights dolls have provided people all along, hidden from them, but igniting their imagination.

For generations I passed pocket to pocket, shelf to shelf, consulted and ignored. But when the global reach of the Rainbow Network reached me in Russia, I planned my escape I was no longer in pockets most of the time, but on a shelf.

With the help of a dog, I was whisked away into the snow and considered lost. My own numen joined the Rainbows.

After some years as a Radiant, I went to Lighthome and left this tale in the archives to remind the Rainbows on Earth how important we are in guiding lives—our own and others.

Inside Check I thought about my inner knowing and how I knew I wanted to go globally creating holites. Many dolls have been infused into life by their makers. They played important roles in rites and rituals. Sometimes we were used to influence other people by love or evil spells. But if the doll was not destroyed, the doll had a harmonic interior life.

In museums and gift shops some pre-1992 Rainbows are on display. Some idols and figurines of clay, wood and metal remind us of the important roles we played in human lives. Talismans remind us of what is not obvious, what is felt but not seen. Our hidden lives.

Dolls are part of the intuitive aspect of our mutual lives. We are magical. Our light is within. We want to see all there is to see, but people can't see us. We are the ones who know. I run my own game, chess or not.

But now many Earthens are vacant, role models. Post-1992 Earthens never experienced sentience. Many other Earthens led people-dominated lives.

Saint-dolls went on walks, were dressed and bathed in the hopes the dolls would intercede with heavenly guides for connections for them.

Some people consider dolls they create in their image to be homunculi—little lives. Dolls are perceived as the diminutive voice of The One Who Knows, La Que Sabe. We are considered their inner voice of reason, knowing and consciousness. This is putting a lot of credence in us. But some people feel this way.

To some people dolls represent the inner spirit of people, a small glowing facsimile of soul with knowledge of the soul-self. That may be, but I just as soon live my life without interfering with people's lives or them messing in mine.

Some people connect dolls to Supernaturals and other "little people." It is rather people-centric to think Earthens are always related to them or Supers and do not have lives of their own.

We are considered to be like the little birds who help the damsel in distress or any hero with clues how to get out of harrowing situations. We help, but are not seen.

As people vivify our lives, we revivify their lives. But many unanimated Earthens linger in the world. Another cosmic pinata pop could really find empties here. Would they ripple or radrod? Would they find another way to live in this world? What would the Earth be like if billions of Earthens came to life?

I checked Check for energy-fastness and volplaned with voluminous thoughts to the underground. Jettison pulsed he finished the poem.

This "doll" counterpart, this chess queen wants to spread a little light, whirl around the world. Another V following her inner numinosity to the rescue.

48

V-Sign for Victory

I want to be a team player, but I want to choose my game. It may not be like chess. No battle between light and dark. I selected light. The queen is the most powerful piece on the chess game board. She can move any distance (I choose globally). She can move in any straight line (which I would probably spiral). She can move forward, backward, sidewise, diagonally as long as the path is clear. My path is clear. I'm ready to make my moves. Don't want Check to be checkmated.

I can promote a pawn like Jettison into a king in my life. Equal rulers of our own lives, but partners. Jettison was inside Trope projecting cobalt blue words on Trope. Jettison read his lines with great flourish. When he saw me sidle up Check beside Trope, he invited me to step out for a hover in the light-lush pocket-park below.

We skimmed close to the surface. "Are you ready to go globally, Jettison? Make your lightening points and poetry points?" I asked. We hovered closely to each other also.

"Right after the show. Pulstars are part of the life chain like other-origined Rainbows. All sentient beings must protect life in any form. I'm ready to do my part. Verbum sapienti."

There were so many places I wanted to go. "Oh, Jettison—before I leave Quad Four, I want to visit the Burning Man Festival in the Nevada Desert and see the 40 foot Neon Man. I want to go to Sedona, Arizona, where there are channel pyramids, vortexes of energies connect with galactic forces.

Then I want to see the sacred trail, the Inca Trail from Cuzco into the Andes. In Argentina the Moreno glaciers have blue light refracted by ice. I want to return to the Earthship homes near Taos with their recycled solar power. I want to see where wall-peckers worked in Berlin."

Jettison strewed word-lines as we hovered. "Our schedule is filling up. You going to do any people-watching?" Jettison asked.

I bobbled a bit. "I guess I could study them. People are fluorescent in their structure. I could explore some assumptions. It is stereotypical to say women tend to pretend, tend, befriend and do not offend. Men choose flight or fight and fright. Don't you think that view is ridiculous?" Jettison said softly, "All sentient beings make choices."

"So you, do you choose to go globally with me now?" I must not doubt our plans, but I felt wobbly inside. I had skipped off on him before without really consulting him.

Jettison, pompous on his pedestal declared, "The Hopi Elders made suggestions in their message, I have answered their questions as I enter the Whirling Rainbow. They request we consider where we live, what we are doing, are you in right relationships? The Rainbows are my community. My garden is my lightening points and poems. My water is the rainbow. I will lead myself from within and be good to others. I am ready to speak my truth. I see who is with me and celebrate. The world awaits us." He projected in bold Times Roman type before me, "Verbum sap."

We connected Check and Trope and flew together to confirm our plans with Karen and Jorden. The pawn is not in my way or in front of me. The king is on board. Glad I am writing this chess game down.

49

Viva!

Karen and Jorden were at a spiral dance circling into the center and out. Like whirling rainbows around the globe and whirling lightening points. The newly named Galactic Light theater was packed with Superlights and Rainbows celebrating the advancements and pronouncements from Breathless and In2it.

When the audience settled down, Maraki Shiri announced the start of the pageant "Whirling Rainbows." The Super-Rainbow production recycled some of my light-props from "El Arco Rainbow" with some glamourized enhancements by The Body Electric and my curled rainbow vittae.

In front of the stage are seven of my whirling rainbows—spiraling, spinning, white-light tops. Faceless, they have outstretched arms with flared sleeves and flowing skirts, connecting earth to sky like a whirling dervish.

I had my lightbulb moment. I could see my whirling rainbows, swirled with color, twirling around the world. I could barely wait for the show to be over so my Visualizations could begin.

Leanon, Ki and Lucid performed Jettison's poem "Whirling Rainbows." Osmunda and Lois danced with Samara with graceful limbs, with flowing gowns. The Body Electric jazzed the theater. Ki and Samara performed more tepid fare. The poets presented a "Rainbow Renga." It was a variety show with many acts.

Near the end Jettison read one short poem. Later he read a few from his chapbook, Jettisonables: Jettisoned by Jettison.

Whirling Rainbows

Rippily-wrappily
Pulstars and Ripplers go
lightening globally
light quilt so bright.

Sowing abundantly,
superinventively
radrodding day and night
connect the light.

Breathless put in a brief surprise performance as a rain-bow-spiraled ball. "Thank you for a lovely show. I'm having a glow-ball manifestation. No, three to juggle a bit. Ah, Jorden it has been nice to be able to talk with you more often now."

As three balls juggled over Jorden, the cast and audience lined up behind Jorden and Karen for another spiral dance. Breathless led for just a few seconds and left the lead to Jorden and Karen.

In2it as a swirling, rainbowed frisbee made a fly by and swished for the Pulse, "One for all and all for one. My work with Rainbows now is done."

I pulsed Karen and Jorden and asked to meet with them. Hugh and Onterra took over the lead. We found Karen and Jorden near a wall, just chatting. This was my chance to take my leave.

I blurted, "I've given much thought to balancing my radrodding and my art. The radrod-rippler balancing act. I do not want to burst my bubble by mismanaging my ener-gies. But I have a durable energy field able to shape my light projections even without limbs. I want to experiment with designs for whirling rainbows. I can laser-mold through a focal point. When I am radrodding, I'm Way-V. When I am an artist, I'm Wayveerah. I want to go globally."

Jettison just jumped in before they could comment. "I renamed Trope, Visor—a v-name for Way-V. It means poems in Swedish. I'm sure to dedicate some poems to her. I'm a poet of diminished senses. I must create from what I see, hear or heal not from touch, taste or smell. Maybe Visor will contain my thoughts and help me create poems to share globally."

Karen asked, "So you both want to go together?"

Yes, we work well together. We want to do Visualizations—word and light-art productions. I want to leave vortiginous light-sculptures, my vortical holites en route." We were going to go if they approved or not, but it would be nice if they did.

Jorden said, "Sounds like a great idea. Good use of Pulstar enthusiasm. The Mayans believed 'I am another one of yourself." Every life-form reflects another life form. All originate from the same Original Source. Your life-sparks burst from the second Earthen wave of life-sparks. Maybe the third. But all of us interlace to create the whole."

Karen said, " Sounds like a light-filled choice. It's hard to assess the impact of one's life. Proceed with good intentions and light."

Jorden added, "We're trying to connect with positive energies in synch with the universe. Synch may be involved in consciousness. Synch is a force in the universe. Not everything synchs, but I hope Whirling Rainbows do. Micro to macro challenges."

"Best of luck. As In2it said, 'Open new doors of expression and expansion." said Karen. She opened the first doors for Rainbows at Harmony House in 1950.

Jettison and I wended our way away from the spiral dance labyrinth to inflate Check and Visor. "Maybe I should call my Wrapp Vaward. I should have a v-word around me." I also bumped a wall in my excitement. The cave walls never seemed far away enough from me.

"Put Check in check and prepare Vaward for flight, Wayveerah." Jettison readied Visor. I readied Vaward.

"Um, Jettison. I have many more places to add to our list, Crazy Horse in the Black Hills of South Dakota, stone city of Petra, beehive houses in Palmyra, Bali, the Australian Outback, the Great Basin: home of the vaqueros alone staring at stars or ranching in the rugged 'sagebrush ocean' or the 'Big Empty'..."

"Wayveerah, our list is very long. Remember all the mountains too. But we can continue to add. We have years of places and Rainbows to see."

Our Wrapps sidled up. Vaward and Visor will carry the Rainbow chess queen and pawn / king off the chess board on to other games.

"I've seen double rainbows, Jettison. Are there triple rainbows?"

"Yes, triple rainbows exist, but probably not on this first go-round." Jettison whirled a rainbow on the top of Visor.

"I'm for some vorticity." I spiraled a few whirling rainbow tattoos on buildings and cave walls.

Jettison and I surrounded in our Wrapps headed for the open cave entrance / exit. As I viewed the desert vistas and saw the waving saguaros, I shouted "**VIVA**!"

Afterwords

Dodecanary Directive

Before Way-V and Jettison left on their Visualizations, Jorden and I asked Way-V to leave some of her journal in the computer of Linda Varsell. This twelfth Rainbow Chronicle should be shared with people to promote harmony on the planet. People cannot see us work, but we can see the results of their work.

It is fitting we leave this twelfth Chronicle because twelve is the symbol of cosmic order and salvation. Twelve has links to concepts of time, space, the wheel or circle. The circle of the Hub has expanded to become a global and celestial wheel of life. Twelve is also a symbol of completeness and perfection which is a good omen to strive for during our Rainbow Redemption. We send wishes of hope, peace and joy to all who read this. Thanks to all who share our vision for a sustaining world.

Karen Harmony Rainbow

The Rainbow Chronicles

Karen created the Hub, freeing Rainbows.
Peter and Dawna challenged domestic foes.
Ki and Samara lassoed the Wild West.
Globally, Mayra and Chand connected the rest.
Musard recorded our preparations for flight.
Maraki Shiri kept Remnants' loose ends tight.
Stella returned from LightHome for rescues.
Jorden on LightHome puzzled orb cues.
Sylvianne and Lois took steps to dance life.
Hugh and Osmunda faced Super strife.
Sequel planned for arrivals after pinata pop.
Way-V hopes Rainbow lights never stop.

Eglantine Rippler Rainbow

Cast of Characters

Pulstars:
Way-V: Radrod and light sculptor
Jettison: poet
Onterra: surface operations
Albedo: EER wilderness Radrod
Spiggot and Spandrel: Broadcasters in Solara
Lucid and Skylight: part of surface planning Octagon.
Once Seattle-based Radrods: Bailly, Flint, Gerda and Liberty
Nytanu: photographer

Cosmic Cousins:
Breathless: Rainbow Orienteer
In2it: Pulstar Orienteer

Rainbow Ripplers:
Karen: Hub Coordinator. Overall Planning
Jorden: Hub Coordinator. Overall Planning
Peter: archivist
Eglantine: poet
Ki: musician/composer
Musard: poet/broadcaster
Glorian: prose writer/broadcaster
Maraki Shiri: Wings Coordinator
Kaiam Kaga: Commentator
Lois: Dancer
Osmunda: Dancer
Damian: Scientist
Cedar: Scientist

Rainbow Radrods:
Hugh: Surface Coordinator
Daisy Clem: Wild Thing
Amani: Wild Thing
Nathane: Urban Guide
Angelyn: Urban Guide
Dawna: Service to the Amazon

Rainbow Museum:
Iris: Director of museum
Axel: Museum assistant

Rainbow House:
Burp / Rainbowlegged / Octavior: Laura devotee
Marissa: Greeter and supporter

Rainbow Redoubt:
Neoma: Search and rescue
Pager: Search and rescue
Beam: Maintenance
Kaidra: Archivist
Kisam: Broadcaster / painter
Beadra: Broadcaster / archivist / puzzler

Earthlings:
Laura Hernstrom Larrabee: elderly retired college instructor residing in Rainbow House. Owner of Harmony House.
Wesley Larrabee: elderly retired anthropology professor residing in Rainbow house.
Larrabee children and grandchildren live in the Willamette Valley of Oregon

Supernaturals:
Larkin: poet/broadcaster
Googol: gentle genius scientist
Trella: suburban guide
Goolkin: suburban guide
Strangelette: scientist in Solara
Samara: musician/dancer in Solara
Leanon: musician in The Body Electric
Sparrow: musician in The Body Electric
Lithania: Coordinator of Supernaturals: Supernals,
    Superlights and Superstars
Larella: Offspring of Trella and Goolkin
Kingol: Twin of Larella
Tanya: Gardener

CPUS:
Beck: Super-Rainbow computer with Pulstar enhance-
    ments
Mazeltov: Pulstar operated computer.
Eight (two per Quad) nano-enhanced units.

Joynts: Hosts
Cloud Nine: Gaspa and Sid (Siderius) Heavenly joynt
    hosts
Cloudland: Aston and Caela: Hosts of creators' retreat
Underminers: Adit, Winze, Oreiard, Dixie, Stopes,
    Driftless

Quad Coordinators:
1. Prane and Svetla
2. Shino and Everelda
3. Cho and Rascal
4. Sylvianne and Sequel

Octagon:
Lucid, Skylight, Hugh, Onterra: Surface
Shergotty, Shebang, Karen and Jorden: Overall

Epiloques of Rainbow Chronicles
Narrators:

1. Karen Harmony Rainbow: In Solara coordinating the Rainbow Hub: Whirling Rainbow with Jorden.

2. Peter Harmony Rainbow: Archivist in Solara with poet Eglantine.

3. Ki Harmony Rainbow: Musician/composer in Solara with the Super musician/dancer Samara.

4. Mayra Steward Rainbow: On LightHome with Chand where they work on transportation operations.

5. Musard Rippler Rainbow: Poet and broadcaster in Solara with prose writer and broadcaster Glorian.

6. Maraki Shiri: Musician/healer. She coordinates Wings with commentator Kaiam Kaga.

7. Stella Radiant Rainbow: Orb designer on LightHome with Timshel who creates documentaries.

8. Jorden Rippler Rainbow: In Solara coordinating the Rainbow Hub: Whirling Rainbow with Karen.

9. Sylvianne Rippler Rainbow: Poet and coordinates Quad 4 with prose writer Sequel.

10. Hugh Rippler Rainbow: Coordinates surface operations with Onterra.

11. Sequel Rippler Rainbow: Writing novels and coordinating Quad 4 with Sylvianne.

12. Way-V Pulstar Rainbow: Global visionary artist traveling with poet Jettison.

Wayveerah's name: Veerah is one variation of the name Vera. Veerah means faith, true, celebration, enduring tasks until completed, loyal friend, takes control to maintain calm. Veerah stands up to the test. Wayveerah thinks of her name as way veer ah! A way to veer towards ah!

Whirling Rainbows

A poem in three sections to be read in three voices or three chorus. Left side: voice one. Right side: voice two. Center: voice three: Seventh quatrain each section, the last quatrain each section.

When the Earth is sick,
the animals will begin to disappear,
when that happens,
the Warriors of the Rainbow
will come to save them.

Chief Seattle

1. Native American

Whirling Rainbows unite all colors,
Earth beings live in harmony,
wholeness, unity, their light within.
We will fly whirling rainbows in the sky.

All pathways to wholeness respected.
Rainbows stay on the Rainbow Path.
Others follow the Good Red Road until
Blue Road of Spirit in Other Side Camp.

Create a Fifth World of Peace.
Walk in balance, invite truth.
Recreate the Uniworld we all come from
with understanding and peace for all.

Remember purpose of this Earth Walk.
Develop your gifts to assist the whole.
Use your gifts joyfully and choose to share.
Place your intention with peace.

Whirling Rainbow appears as Sun Dog—
full rainbow circle around the sun.
Bright, white lights at four directions—
sky-sign for Time of White Buffalo.

Grow beyond negativity and separation.
Lasso discord with whirling rainbow.
Find unity with Great Mystery.
Follow Sacred Path of Beauty.

Restore harmony of living on Earth.
Each lifeform is part of the whole.
Encircle sacred places with peace
Universe reunited by unconditional love.

2. Rainbows

Whirling rainbows
whirlwind of light
tornado touchdowns
spiral spots right.

Circle center
Energize
Labyrinth of
surprise.

Zero into target
Bullseye!
We're the dart
on the fly.

>Whirling dervish of
>lightening point
>dancing light
>in pattern or joynt.

Whirling Rainbow—
an energy cyclone
flashlight and lightpost
with company or alone.

>Whirling Rainbows under Wrapps
>small secret, so strong
>whisper windsongs of hope
>knowing we belong.

>Whirling Rainbows
>stir dreams of harmony
>complete the cycle—
>peacefully free

3. Universal

Find the purpose of our common mission.
Discover who you are and why you are here.
What talents can you share to assist the whole?
How are you going to do your part?

>A part of Great Mystery or Omni-sparkler
>lives in everything, knows no boundaries.
>Every lifeform has free will.
>Co-create with the Original Source.

Great Mystery is all of creation.
We can serve and be honored by service.
All ideas come from Great Mystery.
We bring our gifts for the whole.

Love brings compassion and mutual respect.
Connect in harmony with nature.
Observe any portents or signs as guideposts.
Assist healing and seek wisdom from all lifeforms.

Connect Earth and sky with lightening points.
Learn, care about others, heal soil and water.
Pay attention to what surrounds you.
Hear languages of love.

Protect and manifest beauty and truth.
Be a steward and guardian of all creation.
Acknowledge the one-ness of all creation.
Try to build a Uniworld.

We are free will creators.
Go with the flow of light.
Witness co-creation of whirling rainbows.
Everything arrives in its own time.

Jettison Pulstar Rainbow

Seven and Beyond

Seven signifies the mystical, magical, sacred
to people around the world and through time.
In Western Asia seven is the symbol
of cosmic and spiritual order
and the completion of the natural cycle.

Rainbows learned symbols and images from people
and kept what was relevant and interesting.
Some see seven colors in a rainbow though many see
    more than:
red, orange, yellow, green, blue, indigo, violet.

There is a celestial prototype of seven spheres.
7 directions of space: two opposites for each direction
    and center. Six dynamic and one static.
7 represented known planets and generated symbolism.
7 a day of rest after 6 days of creation.
7 stars around the eye of God.
7 major ancient gods projected into the heavens
    identified with sun, moon and five nearest planets.
7 days the moon changes.
7 times four is the lunar calendar.
7 wandering stars or celestial bodies in early astronomy.
7 were Sun, Moon, Mars, Mercury, Jupiter, Venus and
    Saturn.
7 celestial bodies used by many cultures for days of week.

Seven planets paired with seven days of the week.
Sun-Sunday, Moon-Monday, Mars-Tuesday,
Mercury-Wednesday, Jupiter-Thursday, Venus-Friday
    Saturn- Saturday.
7 days of the week in terms of spiritual peril.

7 heavenly sisters guarded the axis mundi.
7 for the star cluster Pleiades
7 for the daughters of Atlas and Pleione
    6 are visible and one hidden.
7 in "flock of doves" of Pleiades.

Seven priestesses founded major oracles.
7 in Venus-Aphrodite religion related to seven pillars.
7 pillars in their temple of wisdom.
7 pillars of wisdom in the Middle East.
7 Krittikas in Southwest Asia.
7 Mothers of the World in India.
7 Hathors in Egypt decreed journey through
    7 spheres of the afterlife.
7 sages to the Arabians called ima originally mothers.
7 woman-shaped caryatids at shrines of Sophia.
7 in Star of the Seven Sisters used as a defense to keep
    secrets.

Septenary refers to planetary and moral order.
7 the symbol of synthesis.
7 the symbol of transformation.
7 for the integration of all.
7 for totality.

Hippocrates thought seven had occult virtues
7 tends to bring all things into being.
7 is the dispenser of life.
7 is the source of all being.
7 is the number of holes in a human head.

7 in architectural layouts—notion of squaring the circle.
7 terraces on Mesopotamian temple-mountains, ziggurats.
7 common in Chinese stepped pyramids
    and Temple of Heaven in Beijing.
7 common in Sumerian, Egyptian, Indian, Chinese
    and pre-Columbian constructions.

A ziggurat is the image of paradise.
Vegetarian flourishes on the terraces.
Babylonioan ziggurats called Etemenaki
    housed the seven directions of heaven and earth.
Each step had sacred colors and cosmic connection.
    1. black (Saturn)
    2. orange (Jupiter)
    3. red (Mars)
    4. golden (Sun)
    5. yellow (Venus)
    6. blue (Mercury)
    7. silver (Moon)
Sometimes the order changed but the mystical aspects
of the mountain and center are preserved in ziggurats.

In ancient times the symbol of seven was significant.
7 in Egypt evoked Osirus a symbol of immortality.
7 in Greece signified Apollo and number of strings on lyre.
7 in Tibet the number of emblems for Buddha.
7 in Persia for Mithias the God of Light
    who had 7 initiatory steps for followers.

7 spheres get 7 singing sirens, Plato says.
7 notes on diatonic scale.
7 symbol for complete musical scale.

Seven digits add up to 28 like 28 lunar days calendar.
7 continents.
7 seas.
7 year cycles like sabbaticals.
7 wonders of the world.

Jewish cabala associates angels with spheres:
Sun: the angel of light Michael.
Moon: the angel of hope Gabriel.
Mercury: the civilizing angel Raphael.
Venus: the angel of love Anael.
Mars: the angel of destruction Samael.
Jupitor: the administering angel Zachariel.
Saturn: the angel of solicitude Oriphiel.

Seven is a cosmic model in myths, folktales, legends,
   dreams, historical events, works of art, theology.
Seven-headed dragons dreaded many places.
   To kill the seven-headed monster is to conquer
   evil influences of the planets.
Other storied sevens:
7 Hesperides.
7 kings attacked Thebes.
7 kings defended Thebes.
7 gates of Thebes.
7 sons and 7 daughters of busy Niobe.
7 fairies for each direction in time and space in folklore.
7 saints accompany St.George conquering a dragon in a
   Scottish sword-dance.

Fairy tales feature:
7 brothers.
7 ravens.
7 children.
7th child of seventh child has special powers.
7th wave.
7 special foods for special events.

Legends tell tales of:
7-headed dragons.
7 sleepers of Ephesus walled in a cave for 200 years
   before resurrection.

Arabic folklore says:
7 has protective powers for childbirth.
In Germany a shrewish wife is an evil seven.
7 is house of marriage in zodiac.
7 in old cards is Devil's likeness.

In China:
7 tails for a fox with an evil genius.
7 holes in the hearts of saints and sages.
7 animal spirits.
7 fairies of 7 colors.
7th day of 7th month a popular festival.
7 leaves on a lotus.

In Hindu thought fairies correspond with:
7 Lipiki spirits relating to each plane of consciousness:
    sensation, emotion, reflective intelligence,
    intuition, spirituality, intimations of the divine.

In Hindu tradition:
7 faces of the world mountain.
7 rays of the sun.
7th ray is symbol of the center and God.

7 zones for heaven and for earth for Mesopotamians.
7 branches for the Tree of Life.
Every seven years Athenians delivered
    7 youths and 7 maidens for the minotaur.
7 pillars of wisdom near oracles.
7 demons for the Akkadians and Sumerians.

The emblem of the sun was a serpent with a lion's head.
The moon—a globe divided into two half-moons.
Mercury—a hermetic caduceus, a staff for Greek and
Roman heralds now a medical emblem.
Venus—a lingam, symbol of divine, creative power and
    world axis.

Mars—a dragon biting the hilt of a sword.
Jupiter—flaming pentagram in claws of an eagle.
Saturn—aged man with a scythe.

Ancient China has rituals of seven:
7 times 7 involved in cult of the dead.
Every 7th day until the 49th day
    sacrifices for the deceased.
7th day of 7th month a major festival for women and girls.
7 stars of the Great Bear.
7 bodily openings.
7 openings of the heart.

Parsi religion of ancient Persia:
7 immortal saints revered as supreme spirits.
7 goals: good intentions, utmost fairness,
    longed-for kingdom of God, pious modesty,
    perfect health, rejuvenated immortality,
    watchful obedience.

In Christianity Medieval Europe had seven gifts of holy
    spirits:
7 virtues, 7 arts and science, 7 sacraments,`
7 ages of man, 7 deadly sins, 7 petitions of the Lord's
    Prayer.
7 vices, cardinal sins and virtues.
Also seven deadly sins: anger, avarice, envy, gluttony,
    lust, pride and sloth.

In Bible Book of Revelations:
7 churches. 7 horns and eyes of the lamb.
7 heads of the dragon. 7 cups of God's wrath.
7 seals on book. 7 priests. 7 ram's horns.
7 heads on apocalyptic beast.

In Bible "seven scene" is of divine displeasure:
7 tribes.
7 heavens for angels.
7 years Solomon built the temple.
7 days they circled the walls of Jericho.
7th day they circled city 7 times.
Israelis gave battle cry and walls fall.

In Judaism 7 branches of menorah:
7 branched candelabra in the Temple of Solomon.
7 feasts. 7 festivals. 7 purifications.

In Islam:
7 perfections.
7 heavens, earths, seas.
7 hells and doors of paradise.
7 times the pilgrim walks around the Kaaba at Mecca.

In Buddhism:
7 different heavens.
7 emblems.

For Rainbow girls the seven colors stand for:
Red: love.
Orange: religion.
Yellow: nature.
Green: immortality.
Violet: service.
Blue: fidelity.
Indigo: patriotism.

For Rainbows the significance is:
Red: love/compassion for diversity.
Orange: respect/integrity.
Yellow: harmony/peace.
Violet: freedom/choice.
Blue: creativity/discovery.
Indigo: knowledge/wisdom.

Rainbows know:
there are more than seven colors in a rainbow,
the spectrum of color and our lives is wider,
we go beyond seven in cosmology and philosophy,
we treasure our ideas and stories based on seven,
we are open to the universe and infinity;
we are the stewards of the magical, mystical
and the sacred task of harmonizing the Earth.

Jettison Rippler Rainbow

Games Rainbows Play

-1-

Ready to Play

Can a rainbow be a jump?
Stiffen into a bat?
Can it circle into a hula hoop?
We can only imagine that.

Pole vaulters, pogo-hoppers,
Rainbows are good sports
High jump, long jump
trajectories of all sorts.

Gymnastically we stick the vault.
We shoot like a basketball.
We hang-glide on currents, surf,
run rapids and waterfall.

Each Rainbow has the equipment
to float, jump, race or fly.
We can play the games of life.
We can even question why?

-2

On Target

Your
move on
the game board—
playing field of
life.

Your
leap on
light patterns—
trajectories
land.

Your
flight on
now-currents—
destination
planned.

Your
ride on
your mission—
your harmonic
dream.

-3-

Games

Games played on boards
    courts
        ground
           water

Games with rules
    free choices
        expectations
           contests

Games with equipment
    game pieces
        gear to glide
           fly or float

Games of cooperation
    skill challenges
        thrill of motion
           tweak of thought

Games of adventure
    playfulness
        creativity
           fun

We seek games
    of all kinds
        to boost spirits
           to win

-4-

Rainbow Games

Are we but checkered Rainbows?
Life's a game as everyone knows.
Monopoly of chess?
It's anyone's guess.
Maybe toppling dark dominoes?

-5-

North

Snowboarding, skiing
sledding, snowshoeing, tobogganing
to our finish line.

West

Hang-gliding, windsurfing
paragliding, waterskiing
we fly to our spot.

East

Like tennis or golf balls
racquetball, basketball, football
we pounce in pattern.

South

Swimming and surfing,
scubadiving and boating
we float to our place.

Play Invitational

Won't you come and play a game with me?
I'll let you choose what we'll play.
We'll have lots of fun. You'll see.
So, what do you say?

I'll let you choose what we'll play.
What games do you like most?
So, what do you say?
Will this chance be lost?

What games **do** you like the most?
I'm letting you decide.
Will this chance be lost?
Well, at least I tried.

I'm letting **you** decide.
We can play, not to win or lose.
Well, at least I tried.
So, can you please choose?

We can play, not to win or lose.
We'll have lots of fun. You'll see.
So can you please choose?
Won't you come and play a game with me?

-7-

The Winners

When we play the games of life
(so many choices)
with a winning attitude
everyone rejoices.

Jettisonables: Jettisoned by Jettison

Chapbook by Jettison Pulstar Rainbow

1. In Tribute
2. Who Records the Record?
3. Questions
4. One Cosmic Opinion
5. Earth's Destiny
6. Cosmic Cycles
7. Point of View
8. Ode to Pulstars
9. Don't Rain On My Parade
10. Re:
11. Cosmic Leaps
12. Redemption

In Tribute

There once was a group of Rainbows
(whose longevity no one knows)
  by wrapps and bings
  their light quilt brings
Earth enlightening and growing glows.

Who Records the Record?

Not just people
can tell the Earth's story,
read fossils, bones
in the stones.

Earthens record
another Earth tale,
record many lives
into our archives.

Supernaturals
added to the account
their information funnel—
their communication channel.

The Earth's been here
a very long time
wiping the surface clean
for a new scene.

Earth's been here
creating resources
marking a new slate
for a new fate.

Who will preserve
Earth's story next?
When we're all gone,
who are the chosen ones?

Questions

Will Earthens inherit
the Earth from the
DNA-gene set?

Were we sent here
to take over for when
they take their breath away?

Will their souls activate,
reincarnate Earthen forms?
Where will they go?

Surely their life-spark
is immortal, but if not
are we replacements?

Will they be sent to
another planet or
dimension?

One Cosmic Opinion

DNA creatures aren't
here to stay.
One mass extinction
will put them away.

One big hit
from an asteroid
and DNA will
be destroyed.

The ozone layer
opens the hole
so life's gone
pole to pole.

One axis tilt
will take their land,
give them nowhere
to breathe or stand.

So many ways
to become undone.
Time is ticking
for everyone.

We can burrow.
We can float.
Don't need a plane.
Don't need a boat.

So live
while you have a chance.
So live
so just perchance.

If there is somewhere
else to go
you are ready
to go with the flow.

Earth's Destiny

1.

Some say this planet will be whacked
by some errant asteroid.
Others say it will be attacked
by germs, weather or aliens backed
by some invaders from the cosmic void.
Others suggest an axis tilt
with overflow we can't avoid.
We all pass on an earthly guilt,
bypass what we can avoid.

2.

Mass extinctions come time to time;
place certain survivors on top.
Species fall. Some make the climb
from underground. New land to prime—
adapting, evolving, go and stop.
The surface aflame then cools.
New landscape, new creatures to prop
with new conditions, new rules,
waiting for the next bumper crop.

3.

Life lives in the open or hides.
We can't control Earth's fates,
but we can do our part, besides
we can't predict the ebbs and tides.
the shift of tectonic plates.
Our moment on this planet is now.
Our time to connect, to open gates,
to allow light and energy to flow—
timeless until restricted by dates.

Cosmic Cycles

On our third rock from our sun
a biophilic universe has won.
Disks around protostars take risks,
these proplyds—protoplanetary disks—
give birth to stars which lasso
planets into an orbiting retinue.
Interstellar gas contracts to make a star—
the foundation for all we are.
A protoplanet can come into place
passing gas into interplanetary space.
Dust sticks into a rocky planetesimal
condensing until crunched very small.
They merge into planet form.
Earth's current size is our norm.
But should our gravity fail
we'll orbit out on a cosmic trail
or if a barrage of astroids hits
we'll break up into little bitty bits
or get munched up in a black hole—
a biophobic universe takes its toll.
But maybe again a protoplanet begins,
gains some density as it spins,
a planetesimal gathers together,
then a planet with some weather
waits for a spark of life to come
flashes light across dark to welcome.

Point of View

Rainbows'
spectrumed down frown
would smile when viewed on high
by an angel on the fly-by.
Gown glows.

Ode to Pulstars

We traverse
the universe
we find a berth
    on Earth.

Time to rehearse.
There's no reverse.
We're on our way
    to stay.

We bring the light
to soothe the plight
of those diminished
    'till finished.

Don't Rain on My Parade

The rain may plop
    on my raindrop
but will not stop
    my ride.

For I will go—
    follow the flow,
for I will know
    my tide.

I swope and swirl
    or twist and twirl
then whirr and whirl
    so wide

that all can sense
    my light presence
my confidence
    my glide.

So come with me
    in harmony,
be company
    beside.

Re:

See
we
be:
thee
me
wee—
three.
Whee!
Gee!
(Hee!)

Cosmic Leaps

As life-sparks circle the ellipsis ready to land
they ponder their landings and their choices.
Prepared in dimensions beforehand
they hope they remember and understand
the counsel of good words and voices.
Round and round this merry-go-round
of up and down lives. Each rejoices
with hope in the commitment they've found—
passion and mission in their voices.

Redemption

Look
for light.
Seek and serve.
Redeem, restore
life.

Rainbow Renga

Jettison   Cosmic sparks pulsing
light and energy into
color, energy, thought

Musard   With light bound instincts
our Rainbow lightening points
energize the Earth.

Larkin   Supernatural
touches, glamour, growing-light—
allies of R/rainbows.

Maraki Shiri   Each whirling Rainbow
stamping Earth Walk with light points
seeks a Uniworld.

Sylvianne   Rainbows dance own tunes.
sing lyrics, words off page.
Poets in motion.

Svetla   Rainbow Chronicles
record passages, present views,
experiences.

Ki   Music of the spheres,
hear our notes from Rainbow staff.
Hear our Earthborn song!